In March 1951 Tom Stevens sailed from Southampton aboard the troopship *Dilwara*, one of the last generations of British soldiers to serve in the West Indies. 'How did I get here?', he asks. Tom's candid memoir describes his wartime childhood, disrupted by evacuation, the Swansea blitz, patchy schooling, his father's absence at war and his parents' separation. He evokes with an engaging honesty the life of an infantryman in the garrison of Jamaica, the pleasures of tropical service and the temptations faced by a young man in uniform. Vividly recalled, Tom's memoir reveals how a young Welshman grew up in the final years of colonial Jamaica, recalling the complex relationships he enjoyed with its people. Tom candidly recounts the two amorous adventures that make his account of his time in the West Indies unique: his infatuation with Elvira, the Belize beauty for whom he risked all by deserting to elope with her, and Marcia, the Kingston woman with whom he lived happily, as long as neither mentioned her life as a prostitute. In between, Tom and his Royal Welch comrades relaxed in the bars of Kingston, cleaned up after a tropical hurricane in Jamaica, suppressed a socialist government in British Guiana and guarded the leaders of the free world when they met in the Bahamas, before leaving the bright sunshine of the West Indies to return to the grey skies of post-war Britain. *A Welch Calypso* opens the barrack room door after lights out, evoking the life of the other ranks in one of Britain's last tropical garrisons. As well as describing a now long-gone military world, Tom Stevens opens his heart in a frank reminiscence of a Welsh boy's coming of age.

Swansea-born Tom Stevens grew up in wartime and as a teenager joined the Royal Welch Fusiliers. His service with the Royal Welch in the West Indies forms the substance of his candid and engaging memoir, *A Welch Calypso*. Back in Wales he married Kaye and they had three children, Adrian, Lesley-Anne and Jonathan, migrating to Australia in 1965. While running a shop in the small New South Wales township of Gerogery, Tom became an artist, painting landscapes and scenes from his childhood. Tom and Kaye moved to Canberra, where in the mid-1990s Tom became blind. He now lives in a residential home in Canberra.

Professor Peter Stanley was born in Britain and migrated to Australia with his family in 1966 aged 10. He met Tom Stevens's son, Adrian, at university in Canberra in 1976. After working as a museum historian for 32 years, in 2013 Peter became Research Professor at the University of New South Wales, Canberra. He has published 26 books, mainly on Australian and British military-social history, and in 2011 his book *Bad Characters* (on Australian soldiers in the Great War) was jointly awarded the Prime Minister's Prize for Australian History.

A Welch Calypso

A Soldier of the Royal Welch Fusiliers in the West Indies, 1951-54

Tom Stevens

Edited and introduced by
Peter Stanley

Helion & Company

Helion & Company Limited
26 Willow Road
Solihull
West Midlands
B91 1UE
England
Tel. 0121 705 3393
Fax 0121 711 4075
Email: info@helion.co.uk
Website: www.helion.co.uk
Twitter: @helionbooks
Visit our blog http://blog.helion.co.uk/

Published by Helion & Company 2014
Designed and typeset by Bookcraft Ltd, Stroud, Gloucestershire
Cover designed by Paul Hewitt, Battlefield Design (www.battlefield-design.co.uk)
Printed by Lightning Source Ltd, Milton Keynes, Buckinghamshire

Text and images © Tom Stevens
Introduction © Peter Stanley

ISBN 978 1 909982 67 3

British Library Cataloguing-in-Publication Data.
A catalogue record for this book is available from the British Library.

For details of other military history titles published by Helion & Company Limited
contact the above address, or visit our website: http://www.helion.co.uk.

We always welcome receiving book proposals from prospective authors.

Contents

List of photographs

Preface

One of the many regrets of my life is that I did not carry a couple of journals with lots of blank pages tucked into my kitbag when I set off for the West Indies. Alas, one of the follies of youth is not to realise the wisdom of recording life as it happens. At the age I was when I served in the army I cared more for fleeting pleasure than the future.

Not having the written word before me I only have memory only to rely on. Apart from parts of the description of the hurricane in Newcastle and the names of those killed in the 1953 plane crash, which I have based on the regimental magazine, I have drawn on my recollections of those years. So this book has been written from memories, memories which come back all the more strongly because for the past sixteen years I have been blind. I was a soldier in a proud Welsh regiment, the Royal Welch Fusiliers. This is my story.

Tom Stevens
Kangara Waters
Canberra 2013

Introduction

Tom Stevens's memoir *A Welch Calypso* presents a unique insight into the old British West Indies as its island communities appeared to a British soldier in the decade before independence. While West Indians value the reminiscences of older residents, it is relatively unusual to come across the memoir not only of a soldier, but also of a soldier whose view of island life is seen from the perspective of the barrack room rather than the officers' mess. *A Welch Calypso* does not detail garden parties at Government House or the doings of expatriate British society. As a 'squaddie' Tom Stevens became intimately acquainted with women of Jamaica and Belize. Indeed, his frank and often moving account is virtually the only tale we have from the perspective of the thousands of British soldiers who served in the West Indies in the twentieth century.

Tom's memoir is distinguished by at least three characteristics shared by memoirs of enduring value. First, it is candid. We can only admire his willingness to tell the truth as he remembers his years in the West Indies. He does not flinch at recording the real life of young soldiers on the town in Kingston. Second, it is descriptive and detailed. Tom has strong memories of his time in the West Indies, and he recounts them with the eye of the painter he became, colourfully and vividly. Third, his view is warmly human. Though at first wary of islanders and their culture, he entered into relationships with them, and not just romantic or sexual relationships: he grew to love the warmth of Kingston life and the sociable people he encountered: he will always keep a corner of his heart for Jamaica, the country and its people.

As the memoir of a British soldier *A Welch Calypso* is the most recent in a succession of memoirs written by men of the Royal Welch Fusiliers.* It is part of a grand tradition in British military memoirs, and especially from the Royal Welch Fusiliers. An unusual number of members of the regiment have written and published memoirs of excellent quality and of enduring historical value. One immediately thinks of several well-known books. Most famous perhaps is Robert Graves's *Goodbye to All That*, a classic memoir of the Great War, or officers'

---

* It needs to be said only once that while a 'Welsh' regiment the correct title of the Royal Welch Fusiliers was officially from 1920, 'Welch'. In 2006 the regiment was at last amalgamated with the other surviving Welsh line regiment, becoming part of the Royal Welsh.

memoirs such as Siegfried Sassoon's *Memoirs of an Infantry Officer* or David Jones's 1937 memoir of the Somme, *In Parenthesis*. Then there is Frank Richards's description of service in India and Burma in the first decade of the twentieth century, *Old Soldier Sahib* and his account of the Great War, *Old Soldiers Never Die*. The Royal Welch Fusiliers has been documented in many other less familiar accounts. Michael Glover's tercentenary history of the Royal Welch, lists a dozen other accounts. But except for Frank Richards's, most memoirs have been written by officers. Tom Stevens's *A Welch Calypso* is the latest in this tradition, though it is in many ways independent of it. Tom has not read any of his forerunners' writings. His account too is candid. He too remembers his service in vivid detail. His memoir will also be appreciated by those seeking to understand what British soldiers did in a distant time and place.

Tom spent time in several parts of the battalion and in several of the places in which the Royal Welch served in the West Indies; at Newcastle and Kingston in Jamaica, and in Belize and Guiana, with a visit to Bermuda. He offers perceptive and descriptive vignettes – the litter of a barrack room at lights out, the appearance of the cooks at Newcastle, the inner workings of the MT or intelligence sections: what it felt like to appear on a charge. *A Welch Calypso* offers valuable insights into the texture of the life of a regular battalion of the British Army in the final decades of empire. His account truly compares favourably with that of Frank Richards's of the same experience, in India, exactly fifty years before.

Those who have not seen military service may be surprised at the closeness of the life of a battalion, with its strong sense of community, sometimes comradely, sometimes claustrophobic. Tom's memoir conveys a great deal that is recorded and conveyed in no other way. Even a regiment with good regimental histories and a strong magazine fails to record a great deal of the internal, not to say intimate, life of a regiment. Some is taken for granted: the terminology is assumed to be too ordinary to need explanation. Other aspects might seem trivial, but acquire an importance in retrospect much greater than at the time. Other aspects might be regarded as embarrassing: but not to Tom. His memoir reveals much and conceals very little.

One of the strengths of *A Welsh Calypso* is the author's awareness of the world beyond the battalion. He recalls the colour and vitality of Jamaican life, but also its poverty and the consequences for the men and women of the island. The 1950s was a crucial decade in the history of Jamaica, the first full decade in which Jamaicans were able to vote. The colony gained independence, peacefully, in 1962. Tom's memoir therefore captures part of the final decade of colonial

Jamaica. His relationship with Marcia gave Tom entrée to aspects of Jamaican life usually opaque to soldiers.

The story of Tom's life after the events narrated in *A Welch Calypso* needs to be told. He left the army in 1954, married Kay and lived in Wales, doing various semi-skilled jobs – including a spell as a postman. In 1965 they and their children, Adrian and Lesley-Anne, migrated to Australia, following Tom's sisters (who later returned home). They settled in Gerogery, a hamlet in southern New South Wales, where Kay ran the local shop and Tom the post office, having had another son, Jonathan, in 1968. Here the flair for drawing seen in the intelligence section on Bermuda blossomed. Tom took drawing and painting classes at college in the nearby city of Albury, gaining an Associate Diploma in Visual Arts at the Riverina-Murray Institute of Higher Education (now Charles Sturt University). He won several prizes and found fulfillment in producing oils, especially landscapes of the bush and farming country around Gerogery and a series of paintings interpreting and ruminating on the events of his wartime childhood. Sadly, he painted no pictures reflecting his time in the West Indies. Instead, in 1994 he began a manuscript account of his army life. And just in time: in 1995 his eyesight began to fail and by 1997 he became completely blind.

Tom has met the pain and frustration of blindness stoically and with immense patience. He continues to take an interest in the world through the radio and talking books and discusses more than the weather with intelligence and insight. For a time he continued to write, persisting with primitive, unfamiliar and tedious voice recognition software and winning prizes for his short stories. He is a man of great dignity, whose compassion and humanity shines through this, his story.

I have known Tom since 1977, when I was at university with his son Adrian. Knowing that I had become a military historian, in the late 1990s Tom showed me his memoir, diffidently asking what I thought of it. I had read many British soldiers' memoirs, from India in the nineteenth century to the world wars, and I was able to place this account in a great tradition of British military memoirs. I began to transcribe and edit the manuscript, reading it back to him and making changes. This alone would have made it a slow job, but it was further interrupted by the ups and downs of life. At last, after a decade of on-again-off-again progress, the manuscript was more-or-less complete. It has been a great experience to share the creation of this book with Tom. In doing so I learned lessons about honesty in story telling and clarity in writing that I will always treasure.

A Welch Calypso is a wonderful evocation of a vanished time. It conjures up a world – the last years of empire – which can never come again. It also evokes a time in Tom's life in which he discovered much about himself and about the world. In bringing together the hidden world of the regiment and the forgotten world of Kingston in the 1950s, Tom Stevens has helped us to understand that long lost time and distant place.

I am grateful to Tom for having the courage to tell his story so frankly, to his daughter Lesley-Anne for supporting the production of this memoir in so many ways, and to Duncan Rogers of Helion and Company for consenting to publish it.

Peter Stanley
University of New South Wales
Canberra

1

Now is the hour

'Now is the hour for me to say goodbye. Soon I'll be sailing far across the sea.' Mostly Welsh voices sang the *Maori Farewell* with a mixture of sadness and excitement. It is 1951, in Southampton, England. The First Battalion of the Royal Welch Fusiliers is preparing to sail on its posting to the British West Indies, for a three-year tour of duty. As a regular soldier with over three years to finish my time, I knew I would be leaving Britain probably for the whole tour. The thought filled me with youthful anticipation of what lay ahead.

Twilight was settling over the British Empire, with Britain still keeping a watchful eye on her possessions in the Caribbean. Another five years on – with the Suez Crisis – Britain would no longer be a world power of the first rank, but in 1951 the illusion of greatness still camouflaged the fact of decline. Britain kept a battalion of troops at Kingston, in Jamaica, from where a detachment could be sent to any trouble spot in the Caribbean. The Royal Welch was leaving to take over from the Royal Inniskilling Fusiliers, an Irish regiment that had completed its tour.

It was Sunday, 4 March. His Majesty's Troopship *Dilwara* of 12,555 tons, lay at the quay, anxious to be on her way. Soldiers, covering the deck, pressed up to the ship's rails, watching the activity ashore and singing to the music of the band playing on the dockside. For me, this was the great adventure and I was glad I was not standing in the crowd ashore farewelling the *Dilwara*.

We had left Chester early on the Saturday morning, armed not with our rifles but with a supply of sandwiches packed by the cookhouse for the train journey. The sandwiches were substantial, about an inch thick. They kept us satisfied during the long journey south. As we poured into the carriages, one Fusilier called out to the mothers of the town to unlock their daughters as the Royal Welch were saying goodbye! Before we left camp that morning, I had watched several men running on the railway track near our billet; the general opinion was that they were deserters. I found this difficult to understand, but conceded it was probably so. I wondered why they had left their run so late: perhaps they were hoping to evade detection before the ship sailed. I stood at the window, high above the track, watching the figures until they passed around a bend, still visible through the trees for a short time, before finally passing from view. I turned away to continue preparing for the journey to Southampton, glad to be me and to be going where I was going.

The train journey swallowed up most of that Saturday and we arrived at Southampton docks towards evening. It had been a pleasant enough day, relaxing in the carriage, reading, munching on the sandwiches, and gazing out at the countryside passing by. We were not overcrowded, and the company was friendly, with plenty of humour going around our carriage, some on the expectation of the brown-skinned girls we would soon meet up with in Jamaica, and the possibility of catching a 'dose'. Many National Servicemen, who would have had girlfriends or even wives, may have had different sentiments at the prospect of not seeing home for a year or more. The joking was superficial: a small ball of fear bounced around my insides. At Chester we had been shown films on the perils of sexually transmitted disease, which we knew simply as 'VD' – venereal disease. These films had made an overwhelming impression on me at least. After seeing images of the destructive forces of venereal disease, particularly that of syphilis, I had left the lectures with strong convictions of not being drawn into that whirlpool. What fools we mortals be! I was to find the mating instinct a powerful force indeed in young men so fit and strong. Some time later we were to hear the convincing

The troopship *Dilwara*, taken from a postcard 'Tommy' sent to 'Dad and family' on the eve of departure for Jamaica.

rumour of our tea being laced with bromide, a substance believed to dampen our urges. But if this was indeed the case, I shudder to think of the results without it. It had little effect on me, or others, to the best of my knowledge. Many National Servicemen left Britain's shores swearing to remain true to their girlfriends and wives: some did. Many tried to remain faithful but a lot succumbed to Jamaica's temptations. Today, even with the AIDS virus, sex is not easy to deny. A night on the town, a few rums, and reason went on holiday. It would return only in the morning to come, with vows of abstinence forever on being spared from falling into the abyss of reporting sick. Eventually we came to recognize the first signs of gonorrhea, four or five days after intercourse, a yellowish, thick discharge – known as 'blobbing' – from the penis. Urinating became very difficult and painful. A soldier might say, 'Stuff me, I'm pissing razor blades'. The description said it all. Thankfully I was never to have this experience. How the mind could agonise at the morning pee for up to a week after falling from grace. The relief rising within and escaping in a deep sigh, on the pleasurable and painless stream leaving the bladder and tinkling against the porcelain. It was a game of Jamaican roulette.

All this was in the future. For the present we were still at Southampton, spending our Saturday evening waiting to board His Majesty's Troopship *Dilwara*. We were assembled in a very large wooden holding area at the dockside. The shed (let's call it that) bustled with noise and commands. Nothing seemed to really happen for all of this activity, as we stood in the 'stand easy' position with the blue sea kit-bags we had been given. (Our canvas kitbags were being stowed in the ship's hold.) We waited to move up the gangway of the large white ship, the fat hull of which we could see below the wooden roof of the building. The upper structure of the *Dilwara* stood exposed to the chilly March evening; bright lights reflecting brilliantly in the calm water. We conjectured that we would be confined to the ship this Saturday night, but that officers of the Fusiliers might be allowed a social time ashore.

Then, something began to happen. The ranks were called to attention before moving off in a long, steady line to shuffle upward, to board the troopship. Reaching the deck of the *Dilwara*, the line slowed, as it wound down into the intestines of the ship, before reaching what would be our home for the following weeks. We were to be berthed in a broad deck, with rows of bunks, two or three high to which we were allotted. Once we were all accommodated this impression of space disappeared on the crowded troop-decks. A wave of sounds passed around our quarters as men settled into their space. Laughter rang out as mates came together again. Kit was pushed under the bottom bunks, thankfully rid of for the present. Army boots echoed on steel decks as men moved around getting to know their surroundings. Commands from Non-Commissioned Officers (NCOs) peppered the noise, as they informed us of what was to be done and what was most certainly was not to be done. Questions could be heard all around. 'This bunk taken, is it?' in the peculiar Welsh habit of making two questions out of one. 'Some fucker's dropped their guts': a pungent fart, unwelcome on the crowded troop deck. An English voice breaks through the lilt of the valleys: 'Where's my bloody kit-bag?' A Birmingham voice: 'Hey, Taff, how're we off for fags?' 'Two's up on that smoke, pal': a man asking for a drag on a fag-end. A voice: 'Where's the piss-house, boys?' rises above the hubbub. Soon things settled down into a reasonable order. I looked forward to a night's sleep. It had been an emotional day.

I remember vividly standing in line, waiting for the mess deck to open for breakfast the following morning. It was a blustery March day with occasional glimpses of thin sunshine, but only a small promise of rain. As we stood in the corridor, I for one, felt refreshed after a good sleep, excited by the knowledge that we would sail that morning. We could glimpse Southampton Water through small rectangular windows to our left. The wind outside seemed strong, as spray from the choppy water blew from the top of small waves. Seagulls screeched around the ship waiting impatiently for any rewards to come their way, in the form of garbage dumped from the galley. The floating food waste would bob in the water for moments only, before the grey-white hordes would descend, screeching and squawking and demolish it quickly in a noisy frenzy; leaving grey-white feathers floating in the churned-up sea. No quarter was asked or given in the competition for survival for these birds and those who had already gulped down food attacked those who still possessed it.

Breakfast was a good start to the trip, tasty and presented well in the light trays we were supplied with. It was a novelty in those days to come across trays recessed with compartments for different foods. Contrary to popular belief in my time in the army I do not recollect consistently bad food. Sometimes it bordered on being very good; though never to the standard I encountered aboard troopships and Royal Naval vessels. Everyone was in good spirits (on the surface at least), even those leaving behind their nearest and dearest, though perhaps not the defaulters, in the ship's cells below the waterline.

Most people, after breakfast, found their way above deck to stand at the rail, watching the goings-on at the dockside. Welsh voices drifted into song, sometimes in opposition to the band playing ashore, until the singing, becoming stronger, rose above the music and drowned it for us on board. I can imagine bandsmen not being too appreciative of competition, having been ordered to appear on the breezy dock, to play farewell music to the lucky sods off to meet the sun, as we saw it. Still, they laboured on, as did the singing, moving time toward 11 a.m., when we were due to sail.

It was a typical March day. The wind played havoc with the clothes of those waiting on the dockside. I remember women's clothing blowing about in the stiff breeze. Occasionally the sun would break through grey clouds; lifting the spirit for a short time, before sulking again in the moving swirl of cloud which would cover it. Sometimes the sun was only lightly covered by cloud and the white brightness shone through, filtered as it was, still giving cheer in the promise of the sun breaking out again.

Now the singers and the band were in unison, joining in a great Welsh song, though with English words. The song 'We'll Keep a Welcome', known to make barn-door rugby forwards weep into their beer, soared out from the ship. The bandsmen were probably glad to be playing now on the same side. Those on the dockside – relatives, army officials and friends – braved the cool weather to fare-well us; shouting out words broken on the wind and muffled by the music.

The troopship *Dilwara* was now ready to make for the grey, choppy sea. Seamen efficiently made ready. With surprise almost, the vessel glided away from the quay. The singers sang with fervor now, as the people ashore receded into figures only, with no faces recognisable. 'We'll keep a welcome in the hillside, we'll keep a welcome in the vales. This land will still be singing when you come home again to Wales.' It would be 1954 before I would see that singing land once more.

*   *   *

Only a short time after leaving port we paraded on deck for our first emergency drill, being given instructions on using life jackets; standing on a deck which sloped dramatically down to the unhappy-looking sea. As we tried to imitate the officer tying the tapes on a life jacket, a ship approached with a surprising suddenness, looking a duplicate of our own *Dilwara*. She was moving towards Southampton, passing close enough for us to see the remarkable similarity to our ship. The cry went up, 'There's our sister ship' and so it proved to be. It was the *Dunera*, the ship notorious for bringing interned German-Jewish refugees to Australia in 1940, though I did not know the name of the sister ship at the time.

At the end of the drill we were allowed to go our own way, to wander around the ship. At least, we were free to explore those parts allocated to 'other ranks':

other areas of the ship were reserved for officers and families. Fusiliers stood around chatting, smoking and generally enjoying their freedom. The trip to Jamaica would take three weeks so there was a lighthearted edge to the men's banter. We supposed that there would be few military duties during the voyage. On the deck there was a swimming pool. There was a cinema when the dining room became converted into a picture palace showing the latest films. Regular 'Housie-Housie' (or Bingo) became a feature of the other ranks' lounge, where alcohol was served at times. A library lounge offered letter writing facilities and a peaceful port in the storm for those seeking escape from their own demons. There were also several card-schools going. Military regulations forbade gambling for money: which is not to say that it did not occur. Below decks there seemed to be a persistent smell of oil.

Life settled down into a reasonable existence for us 'free' men. Not so for the prisoners below deck housed – so we heard – far below in the bowels of the ship, close to the thundering of the engines. I wondered if any of the men seen racing on the railway track at Chester were among those in custody. Not that any of us escaped the sound of the engines entirely. It permeated our shipboard lives, waking up, going to sleep, eating, using the toilets, free of it only in the showers.

Soon we approached a group of islands on the Mid-Atlantic Ridge known as the Azores, islands some 1,500 kilometres to the west of Portugal. (The islands belonged to Portugal and still do.) Already we seemed to have reached tropical waters – the drab skies of Britain seeming further away than the true reality. Names were canvassed for those not on any essential duty who wished to go ashore. For some reason, not now clear, I chose not to put my name forward. As we drew close we saw white houses hugging the land giving the impression of a cheerful place, as the sun played on their walls. They were very much unlike rows of houses in Wales, standing in their sorrow and drabness in the shadows of coalmines or industry, dust or fumes choking an already miserable sky, building up with heavily laden clouds, to a steady downpour.

Soon the *Dilwara* became surrounded by small craft managed by swarthy men of Latin appearance. These traders, some standing up in their bobbing boats, began shouting of the bargains they had available, such as watches and rings, with British currency most acceptable. Youngsters on the 'bum boats' as some called them offered to dive for coins thrown overboard; rising to the surface with a wide grin and the coin gripped between white teeth, set against brown skin. Soon it was raining coins, so many going to the bottom, as the young divers strove to retrieve them, but unable to keep up with the supply. The exchange of goods and money was carried out by the use of baskets, drawn and lowered by lines thrown up from the small craft. This took place at the end of much negotiation between the men lining the rail of the *Dilwara* holding up fingers to denote prices and the shouting traders shaking their heads holding up more fingers until the deals were struck. Most of the bargains were cheap indeed, but there would be no after sale service once the ship left the Azores, or even after the bumboats had left the scene. I did not venture to buy anything.

The shore party left to spend several hours sightseeing. It did not sound as though I had missed much. On their return we were told that the reality at close-quarters contrasted with the impression given on approaching from the sea. The little paradise had streets with a collection of various smells, none of which had anything to recommend. Dirty, tired-looking prostitutes had offered their services, mostly rejected even by soldiers facing a long sea voyage. These women had an aroma too, which was not an improvement on that of the streets. From the various descriptions it seemed a backward, dirty, smelly place. Of course, this was in 1951. Things would have changed in the ensuing years.

We were soon underway again, heading now for the New World. There would be the vastness of the Atlantic to combat before reaching Bermuda, the gateway to the Caribbean, between the Atlantic and the Caribbean Sea. This part of the voyage would be the long haul; many days of heaving sea and empty horizons. The intense, lonely feeling of the mid-Atlantic made it easy to imagine the sentiments of Columbus and his men who had crossed this ocean so long before who did not know their final destination. Looking from the ship at the expanse of sky and water, one knew it had always been thus, with nothing changing here other than the weather; just sea, sea, sea and sky, sky, sky. It somehow turned the *Dilwara* into a flimsy and temporary thing and the souls it carried almost silly in their self-importance. Other vessels had passed this way and more would do so again; but the emptiness of this place continued. It would give, on a much smaller scale, some insight for me when in 1969 men passed through space on the way to the Moon. In the scheme of things, the individual does not count for a great deal, in spite of our self-concern.

I also thought of the Atlantic convoys of the Second World War, with ships stalked by the periscopes of the U-boat wolf packs before sudden explosions and screaming men in burning oil. Those terrible days of less than a decade before were so different to our voyage, almost a pleasure cruise.

For most of the trip the weather was fine but on some days the wind whipped spray from the tops of white sea-horses and those on deck felt exhilarated at the play of wind and water on our faces. As the ship cut through the water at night I would watch flying-fish racing through the ship's bow-wave, glistening in the light reflected from the portholes. Standing at the rail, spray carried on the cold wind lashed faces looking out into the blackness; the friendly red glow of cigarettes giving a kind of security to the watchers. The cigarettes spread over the ship like glow-worms. Speech was difficult, as the words were captured by the wind and lost, leaving the ears tingling and a sharpening the senses. I did not suffer too much from seasickness, on this voyage at least. At times I felt some discomfort with the motion of the ship, the thud-thud of the engines and the smell of the oil, but it never became a disabling problem. It would not have been too good for the prisoners below; and I wondered if they were given time above deck to enjoy the sea air.

And so the days passed, beginning with a shave and a shower with salt-water soap (I never found that it lathered). The ship's routine became humdrum and we became lethargic, resenting even the smallest impositions that might intrude into our holiday mood. During our days, music from loudspeakers gave us a diet of the hits of the moment, perhaps played on the 'long-playing' records introduced in 1947. Artists such as Johnnie Ray, Nat 'King' Cole, Al Jolson, Bing Crosby, Judy Garland and Teresa Brewer kept us company through the hours the ship ploughed its way through swollen seas. I also have fond memories of singers such as Vaughan Monroe, famous for 'Ghost riders in the sky', and a Welsh singer, Donald Peers, who sang his hit songs, 'A, you're Adorable' and 'Powder your face with sunshine'. There were endless games of Housie, a mindless pastime I have never been partial to and avoided most of the time. Sometimes, weather permitting, games took place on deck, usually supervised by an officer, with relaxed authority. Time spent at the converted cinema was always good value and well attended. I always would find it so. The silver screen had the mass appeal of the most popular art form of those times, still passing through the big studio and big star era, which many consider the golden years of Hollywood.

Every day the ship's officers ran a sweepstake or a competition to guess the number of nautical miles the *Dilwara* covered in the previous 24 hours. Each day took us nearer to Jamaica.

The Atlantic crossing was nearing its end. Early one sunny morning, in a wonderfully calm sea, we moved past grand white or cream houses close to the water's edge as the British colony of Bermuda told us we were about to enter the Caribbean. I recall how these fine structures reminded me of 'Tara' the home of Scarlett in *Gone With The Wind*. The *Dilwara* seemed to sail forever past these places with grounds coming all the way down to the water's edge. We were heading for Hamilton, capital city of the colony, about a thousand kilometres from the American mainland. Bermuda, even in 1951, leaned heavily towards American culture and to cater for those brash tourists with wallets bulging with 'greenbacks'. It is almost tropical, situated as it is on the edge of the Caribbean Sea and carried much appeal for American honeymooners, anxious to get away from it all, to a place not too far away yet with a sense of being abroad and with reasonable sunshine. It's interesting to note that since those long off days the people of Bermuda have voted to stay under the British flag, in the Commonwealth.

Orders had been issued some days before our arrival informing us of the march the battalion would carry out on the island. We would march, to 'show the flag', in our darker and heavier home-service uniforms rather than our tropical kit. The march was probably aimed at stirring up sea-weary soldiers into a state of readiness more appropriate to military men as much as to impress the Bermudans. Panic prevailed when our home-service tunics had to be retrieved from our kit bags to be cleaned and pressed to an acceptable standard. The voyage had softened us up and I for one looked forward to 'swinging those arms' and stretching our legs on dry land. It was to be a full battalion march, complete with band, goat and pioneers.

But it was a fairly untidy affair compared to our normal standard – I don't think our uniforms were even pressed. I don't remember whether we even wore our white feathered 'hackles' in our berets, one of the Fusiliers' regimental distinctions. I am certain that our boots were not 'bulled' to their best shine.

It was a sunny but cool day and some of the watching tourists must have been uncomfortable in their Bermuda shorts. Many spectators, probably mostly Americans, stood photographing and even filming as we marched along Hamilton's streets; the band playing 'Men of Harlech' and 'The British Grenadiers', with a rendering also of 'Colonel Bogey'. This popular military air, to us certainly, did not have much to do with any colonel. Our version of the refrain did not stand on ceremony: with a chorus of 'Bollocks, and the same to you'. As we marched, I am sure many said these words mentally to the fine playing of the band.

The sergeants marching alongside us gave us their usual chorus: 'You're out of step, you bloody fool', 'Get those bloody arms up', 'Shoulders back', 'Straighten those arms' and 'Bags of pride, boys, bags of pride'.

The large soldier with the leopard skin on which sat his drum, covered in the names of the Royal Welch Fusiliers' battle honours, belted out the steady rhythm in the best of military traditions. The drum, of course, goes back a very long way in the history of man. It has a deep-rooted appeal that stirs emotions buried deep in time, bringing a universal response, from the Red Indians of America to the once-savage tribes of Africa. It appealed to the once-savage Celts too: I always found a quickening of the blood when moving off on parade with those first drumbeats. The Drum Major led the band, flamboyantly twirling his mace. Bravely at times he would throw the mace high in the air and catch it while marching. Many wondered if he would drop it, but he never did.

For many Americans, British soldiers would have been a novelty, but I imagine it would have been astounding to see them being led by a goat. The Royal Welch Fusiliers marched on parade behind a goat. Traditionally named 'Billy', he was – and is – not a mascot, but is considered as being on the strength of the battalion. A common belief was that Billy ate two cigarettes daily. Welsh regiments traditionally had goats on their strength. The Welsh Regiment's were always called 'Taffy'. The Welsh Regiment no longer exists by that name, nor the South Wales Borderers. This regiment, well known as the 24th Foot, won a swag of Victoria Crosses at the defence of Rorke's Drift during the Anglo-Zulu War.

Billy was followed by men in white aprons carrying ceremonial axes gleaming in the sunlight – the battalion's pioneers. Traditionally the pioneers were the men who cleared the way on the march. They were still responsible for minor engineering work in the battalion and were big men. Their sergeant was the only man in the battalion permitted to wear a beard. Each man of the battalion wore the famous black 'flash' unique to the Royal Welch fastened to the back of their collars. Even though we were not up to customary standard I must admit to feeling sensations of pride marching that day, with a show of smartness to each group of tourists at the roadside. I think we all felt that we should put on a good show in front of the Americans.

We were allowed a night on the town that evening, but Hamilton, though clean, turned out to be a very sterile place, I thought. I recall spending a dull time in an American Servicemen's club, before thankfully returning to the ship. Prospective female company was thin on the ground and not particularly interested in poorly paid 'blow-ins' departing the next day. Perhaps we were not aware of the places to go, but I found Bermuda as exciting as watching paint dry.

Soon we were on our way, sailing now in the deep blue of the Caribbean Sea. Men stripped down to wallow on the warm deck in the friendly sunshine. For me, this was the beginning of a golden tan that would be a part of me for the next three years, a love affair with the sun I have never lost. Later on, watching the new drafts from Britain arriving with their pasty complexions, we seasoned 'old soldiers' took a private joy in telling them to 'get their knees brown' before they could speak on any matter with authority. There was not much awareness in those times of skin cancer. In the West Indies even company orders would specify 'Dress: buff order' and we would wear beret and shorts but no shirt.

The ship reached Cuba, visible in a shimmering haze. The *Dilwara* was not scheduled to call there, with only a short distance remaining to reach Kingston. Racing through a calm sea we watched porpoises enjoying the chase alongside. Now we were in the seas of Drake, Nelson and the Welsh scoundrel, Henry Morgan. Sailing here had a surreal quality, as not too many years before I had sat in a dark cinema in Swansea, watching swashbuckling pirates sail the Spanish Main in glorious Technicolor; films of the ilk of *The Black Swan*, starring perhaps the best screen swordsman of the time: Tyrone Power. I could see no galleons on the horizon, but this certainly was the Spanish Main and the Technicolor was all around us.

But most of us were not to see the crowded streets of Kingston just yet. An advance party only would disembark there and the *Dilwara* would then proceed to Belize, British Honduras, on the coast of Central America. Here, there would be a changeover between a company of Royal Welch Fusiliers and one of the Inniskilling Fusiliers, before returning to Jamaica for the main exchange of personnel. What we saw of Jamaica on our first arrival, from the rails of the ship, was the sprawling but still beautiful city of Kingston. A fine city of modern build-ings was surrounded by a much poorer wooden shantytown on a large plain at the foot of a mountain range known as the Blue Mountains. Jamaican dockhands sweated in the warm sun, the droplets glistening on dark brows. I noticed the range of colour on these people, from a real 'African' black to a very light brown. When they conversed, it was at first difficult to make out the speech, even though it was English. At least, the words we were able to understand were. The rest of it, in voices rising and falling in extreme variation, was beyond us. But one word – 'Ras' – figured a great deal in the excitable exchanges. In a way, the speech had the singsong cadences of the Welsh and as we were to find in the days ahead the Jamaicans loved music and singing (although of a different vein) in a similar way. These people had been oppressed since the long decades of slavery by their white masters and there was an affinity with Welshmen who understood.

Our trip to Honduras took a couple of days, with life aboard ship continuing much as it had. Arriving at Belize the shallow water prohibited the *Dilwara* from docking in close. Small craft from the mainland carried our company ashore and brought the Irishmen to the ship. We stood amazed as the Inniskillings came aboard. They were undisciplined, wild and generally inflamed with alcohol. We later learned of their partiality for drinking the clear solvent of Brasso, a polish used to clean cap badges, brass buckles and buttons. To us, imbued with the habits of home service, seeing these men, including NCOs, in such a state made us wonder on the perils of service in the Caribbean, or at least, Belize. I was to return to Belize and would discover perils of a different kind.

The Royal Welch company took its leave and the *Dilwara* pulled out to the open sea, with our Irish friends still celebrating around the ship. Almost before we knew it, we were back at Kingston, ready for disembarkation. As a member of 'C' Company I was to be stationed not at Kingston, but up in the Blue Mountains at a place called Newcastle. Climbing into three-ton lorries, we embarked on our journey to the mountains. The lorries sped along the plain for some fifteen minutes before the gradual climb up the twisting mountain road – there are dozens of bends in it. We passed many dilapidated wooden shacks, the homes of poverty-worn Jamaicans sitting outside, watching our passing with some interest. Young, barefooted children, with huge grins, made half-hearted attempts to race after our vehicles, their screams lost in the noise of the trucks changing gear to meet the challenge of the steep incline ahead. I have wondered since if one of those kids might have been Bob Marley. He had been born in 1945, the son of a Jamaican mother and a British officer. He was to change Jamaica's music from calypso to reggae and introduce reggae music to the world.

As we climbed the mountain road we passed lush, green vegetation growing among the fertile soil of the valleys and hillsides. The Blue Mountains, I have learned since, is famous for its coffee and the coffee liquor, Tia Maria. Behind us we left the fumes of vehicles doing their best and also Kingston spread out on the plain. In the far distance, the still sea met the horizon stripped of clouds and bearing a large ship sailing from the island.

The journey took the best part of an hour, ending suddenly as we came into Newcastle camp situated on the mountainside but divided in two by its large, flat barrack square. One moment we were struggling up the mountain road, then we were passing a large, wooden building on our right, which we came to know as our company stores. This building stood at the beginning of the narrow roadway that opened up to the vast, tarmac covered square, which gave an awe-inspiring view of Kingston. We were to discover the nights would give this view a magical quality as the many lights of Kingston sparkled below. Looking closely, it was possible to pick out the headlights of cars moving through the streets of the city. It was a view that was to become so much part of our lives.

At the right-hand side of the square, as we drove in, I noticed two ancient cannons in front of a wall covered with the sculpted badges of British regiments (the previous occupants of Newcastle). At the side where the wonderful view was visible, we could see barrack rooms following the mountain down.

We tumbled from the trucks, sweaty and dust covered. Lining up on the square, to await our orders, I realised that the journey from Britain had come to an end. This was the beginning of three years, spent mostly on this island and of memories that would stay with me to the present day.

Tom (right) and a fellow member of the camp police at Newcastle, in front of the badges of regiments that had garrisoned Jamaica before the Royal Welch.

2

How did I get here?

I had grown up in Bonymaen, in Swansea, a town then, now a city. My childhood had been changed abruptly by the war. It is not a easy story to tell, but it needs to be told. I was born at 4 Maria Terrace, Swansea, South Wales, on 25 March 1932. My father was Brinley Stevens – he had no middle name – who worked in the Dufferin Steelworks, Morriston; my mother Hetty Newcombe. I believe that she had worked as a house cleaner at Bonymaen ('the place with the big stone' in Welsh – unfortunately I do not speak Welsh but had the odd smattering of the language).

My mother and father took me to the slate-roofed Canaan Chapel in Pentrechwyth to be christened. Naturally, I cried. My father became upset. The minister, who could not have been very used to babies, suggested that they take me to the vestry at the rear of the church. My father, rather hot-headed, said that if I wasn't going to be christened in the church then he'd take me home – and he did. The Stevenses were not really a chapel-going family, though we children attended the Canaan Chapel Sunday School later.

My grandfather and grandmother came from Woodfardisworthy in Devon. The story that the family told was that he had been poaching in Devon and he got into trouble. He took a boat and rowed to Swansea, got a job as a platelayer and sent for my grandmother. She was his second wife. He had had a wife in Devon and had a couple of children. He had thirteen children with his second wife, Sarah. She had a growth on her cheek, like an open sore – I can remember it well. She picked at it and picked at it and (I believed) got cancer. She died in 1941, actually of cerebral haemorrhage. He died in 1943. At 11 I went to his funeral, representing my father, who by then was away with the Pioneer Corps. The night of the funeral I had the most terrible nightmare – of a black angel – as I remember it – I can't remember the details of the dream but I remember the terrible oppressive feeling of it.

My relatives were quite enterprising people. My uncle Elijah owned a grocer's-cum-a-bit-of-everything shop in Pentrechwyth selling staples such as candles and potatoes, which he had taken over from my grandfather. At one time my grandmother ran a bake-house – not a bakery. People without an oven would pay to

26

Hetty, Barbara
(left), Dorothy and
Tom, c. 1940.

Brinley Stevens as a corporal, probably
in 1943, a photo he sent to his son,
Tommy, in 1945.

bake bread in trays with their names on them. Behind the shop my uncle and grandfather had a plot of land where they had a market-garden or small-holding, growing vegetables and even raising geese, ducks and pigs. They had a horse and cart and went down to the railway station a few times a week to carry parcels ordered through catalogues. Alongside the shop there was a row of houses. We lived in the row of houses besides the shop in Pentrechwyth Road: and that was where most of my accidents happened.

I had a succession of accidents and illnesses: indeed I was accident-prone as a child and the various accidents help me to remember ages and places we lived. I swallowed a penny and had to wait for it to come out. I walked into my father when he was carrying a saucepan of hot water and was blinded by scalding water when I was a toddler. My eyes were bandaged for three days and there was some doubt whether I would see again. I did see and would wait sixty years before I actually did go blind. Another time – I was told I was two – my father and I went to my Uncle's shop and I insisted on carrying a large bottle of pop. I fell and cut myself and had to have stitches. There were other accidents – I burned my foot when I walked across a smouldering rubbish heap. I know I was very young when I swallowed the penny and I wasn't much older when I ran into my father. But I was a lot older when I fell off a swing and broke my collar-bone and was a bit older again when I nearly died from diphtheria. At least I survived.

We went to concerts at Canaan Chapel. In one I dressed up in a red uniform and carried a wooden rifle. Once a little girl named Thomas dressed up as a little butterfly in a yellow outfit with wings and was very excited. Houses had front doors that opened straight onto the street. She opened the door and raced across the road to get to the concert. A car hit and killed her: a very sad event. That had a big effect on me. She was such a lovely little girl. Later in life, after I became a painter I painted many incidents I remembered from my childhood and I wished that I had painted that.

Around 1938 we moved to a house that was very poor. I remember that on Christmas Day, one of my presents was a wooden fort – for some reason I put it on the fire. Why or how I did it I don't know. Perhaps because this house had been condemned, we then moved to a brand new Council house in Bonymaen – near the beginning of the war. Father was still working in the steelworks. Mother kept house; few women worked unless they could help it. I didn't know any woman in that row of houses who worked. Father was a charge-hand in the furnace. He had started there as a laboratory boy. He would have been on a reasonable wage and he worked all through the depression. I know that when he was very young he had pyorrhoea. He went to the dentists to take them all out at once, had false teeth put in straight away and had the same set of teeth the rest of his life.

My father stood up for us. Once I threw a ball into the garden next door and the man living there refused to give me the ball back. I remember looking down from an upstairs window watching my father and the man next door fighting in the front garden, with all the people in the street watching. My father was a hero even before the war. Coming home from work one night he saw a house on fire, with children in the bedroom window. He ran in to climb the stairs to try to save them but burned both his arms and the children perished. Apparently, the parents had gone out to the pub and left the children alone at home with candles.

My mother took me to the doctor when I was poorly with a sore throat. The doctor gave my mother medicine but the sore throat persisted. My mother in desperation took me to Swansea Hospital. There they did a swab and found I had diphtheria. I was put into an isolation ward. Any toys I took in I could not bring out. I recall the terrible pain but was in a bad way – it was touch-and-go.

I started school at Pentrechwyth Infants School at the age of three – I know this from checking the register. I can remember the layout of the school and the playground. There was a cloakroom and a large oblong hall wooden floor, with a picture of St Francis of Assisi on the wall– a saintly man with animals and birds around him. All the classrooms were arranged around the hall.

The war that began in September 1939 was to dominate my childhood: my life, perhaps. Father joined up in 1940, about the time of my eighth birthday. There was some doubt about whether he volunteered or was called up – as a steelworker he did not have to go. This led to another accident. I was sitting in the kitchen not long after he had joined and was showing visitors how soldiers saluted. As I brought my hand down I struck the handle of pot of hot stew, spilling the hot liquid all over my arms and legs. I was wearing a woollen jumper and the boiling liquid stuck the wool to my skin. They put me on the kitchen table and smothered me in butter (the worst thing you can do, but it was what they believed was best at the time). I still bear the scars on my legs.

When I left infants at Pentrechwyth I went to Cwm School but it was bombed. Buses took children to Llansamlet School (two buses, leap-frogging to collect children). I never liked Llansamlet – in fact I hated it: I don't know why, perhaps because of the strictness of the teaching. I remember once we were given composition homework and the teacher said that we weren't to ask parents for help. Mother actually helped made me spell work out but I was punished anyway – caned for making mistakes.

I was in Swansea during the terrible three-night blitz, 19-21 February 1941. Swansea city was flattened. It took a real pasting – people living eighty kilometres away could see the flames. We had an Anderson shelter in the back garden (made of corrugated iron protected by earth), which was safe enough except from a direct hit. Our air raid shelter was right outside the back door, only a yard or two from the house. If the house had been hit and had fallen onto the air-raid shelter it would have been crushed. Perhaps the idea was that we could get to the shelter as quickly as possible. The government had sent the materials and father built it. He dug a big pit and erected the corrugated iron over it, then piled earth on top of it. It was cold inside and dripped with condensation. Mother didn't like our shelter and often went into other people's shelters. It was a different time to now: people seemed to be closer in those days, more sociable. Neighbours would stand on the doorstep talking for hours. 'Come into our shelter tonight', they would say.

We spent a lot of time in other people's shelters. I remember being in the shelter reading the comics *Dandy* and the *Beano*, by the light of a candle. You'd hear the

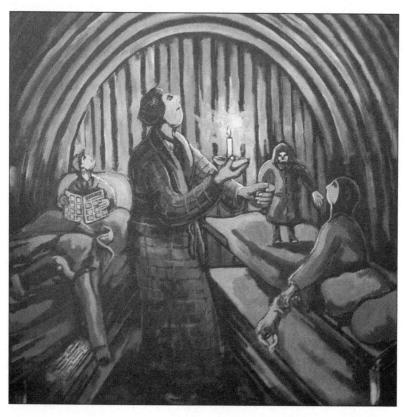

A detail of Tom's later painting of his family in the Anderson shelter during the blitz.

German planes coming over – their engines had a peculiar sound, different to British planes. We would hear the anti-aircraft guns at Jersey Marina firing and we would sit there with our hearts in our mouths.

The nearest we came to being bombed out was when a landmine landed about fifty yards from our house on open ground. Any closer and our Anderson shelter would not have saved us. The explosion caused cracks to appear in the walls of our house and broke crockery. A couple of smaller bombs landed a bit further away and did not go off, but were detonated by army bomb disposal engineers. A few people were killed in Bonymaen. Kids said that bodies had been taken away in pieces in sacks: perhaps they were. The story I heard was that a group were playing cards. They decided to leave where they were and go to another house and as they went down alleyway a blast took them all. My Auntie Alice – my father's older sister, who lived in the next street – told she had a bomb land in her front lawn but it didn't go off. The army bomb disposal men must have seen to it. The crater filled up with water and made a huge lake. People used to drown unwanted cats and puppies in it, as they did in those days. One day a little boy drowned in it – my mother thought it might have been me.

Tom's later painting, depicting his mother fearing that the boy drowned in the flooded bomb crater was Tom.

In May 1940 my father joined the Auxiliary Military Pioneer Corps (later the Pioneer Corps). He was soon posted to 150 Company and reached the rank of sergeant within a couple of months, a sign of his maturity I suppose. In November 1942 his company formed part of the Allied force that took part in Operation 'Torch', the invasion and liberation of French North Africa.

In September 1941 my elder sister Dorothy and younger Barbara and I were evacuated to Pembrokeshire, West Wales. We went by train to the village of Crymych. There we were split up. Dorothy went with one family, Barbara to another and I went to the Thomases on their farm at Penlan. I wasn't very happy there. They were very strict, reserved people. Every Sunday afternoon they would take me to visit Dorothy, whose house was not far away, but I never saw much of Barbara unless we were in school in the village. They gave me a packed lunch for school, but I usually ate it on the way to school. Whether this was this greed or hunger I don't know.

The Thomases lived deep in the country, miles from any town. I encountered things I had never before experienced. Once, I remember, I went with a man working for the Thomases, who went around the place checking rabbit traps. He took a rabbit out of a trap. 'Mind that', he said, but I let the rabbit go. That was embarrassing, but I was terribly ashamed of another episode. I put one of the Thomases' cats into the pond, thinking it could swim. (I was only 9 – I thought cats could swim.) It swam for a while, then it sank. What was I to do? I was terrified and hid the cat's body in the barn. They found it sooner than I expected and I was in deep disgrace.

Eventually the three of us came down with some spotty disease: not measles, not chicken pox, possibly scabies. (The Thomases were more devoted to Godliness than cleanliness.) We were sent to a clinic, away from other children. Mother and father came to see us and gave the three of us a big box of sweets: I don't think we got much else. Soon after we were then taken back to Swansea. By this time the raids had well and truly stopped. I didn't have a pleasant time as an evacuee but Barbara had and she stayed in touch with the family she had lived with and even went back to stay with them.

Around this time, 1942, Mother went to work as a conductress on the buses and we children were often forced to wait for her to come home. We were sometimes on the streets waiting for her to come home at all hours. In 'double summer time' it was still daylight at 10 at night. So we would play outside, hopscotch and so on. But it was not very nice having to wait for hours, especially if you were hungry. But the worst effect of her working on the buses was that she met a man: a common enough story in wartime, I suppose. He was Ben Francis, a military policeman, aged in his late thirties. (He had an easy war.) She met him on a bus. I don't know if he kept asking her out but eventually she started going with him. Later she began bringing him home – which also wasn't very pleasant. I was young but we children knew that this was not right and it changed our lives forever.

I had a lot going on in my mind, what with Dad away, Mum carrying on and not liking school. I began what we called 'mitching' – truanting. Instead of going to Llansamlet school I would go up Kilvey Hill, walking aimlessly. It was actually more of a mountain – or so it seemed to me. Eventually I would come to Swansea and roam about the streets. One day I went into the British Home Stores to look at records. I got to the top of the stairs and there was Ben Francis and my mother. She looked up and we saw each other instantly. I fled, too terrified to go home. I hung outside the back door for hours but at last I had to go indoors. There was Ben. He took off his leather belt, took me upstairs and belted me. It hurt, but what hurt more was that he wasn't my father and had no right to hit me. My mother let him do it. You can imagine that I didn't like him very much.

Later in 1942 things got worse. My mother got pregnant to Ben and had the baby at home in bed in the parlour. I told her 'I'm going to tell Dad about this when he comes home. What a terrible thing you've done. He'll sort this out,' I said. She became violent and went to hit me with the poker.

Of course in a community like Bonymaen it was impossible to keep such a thing secret and my dad found out. My Auntie (one of my dad's older sisters) lived across the street and she obviously knew about Ben Francis. He found out about the baby and stopped writing to mother. By this time he had served in North Africa and in 1943 went on to Italy. We got news of him in another way. On Christmas Eve 1943 we read on the front page of the *South Wales Evening Post* that he had been Mentioned in Despatches for having captured a group of German paratroopers, soon after the invasion of North Africa.

My mother and Ben named the baby John – my half-brother. (He died of a heart attack aged 62, very overweight, apparently sitting up in bed having a glass of whiskey and a cigarette – he had been a tobacconist.) My mother must have found this situation very stressful. She said that she was going away for a couple of weeks to Birkenhead, Cheshire – where Ben Francis came from – and my sisters and I were to stay with a neighbour, Mrs Edwards. She did not return and Mrs Edwards must have gone to the authorities, who decided what would happen to us. My younger sister Barbara went with an Auntie on mother's side – and me and Dorothy went with Auntie Alice in Bonymaen. Towards the end of the war mother left us for good to live with Ben Francis. I've always thought that this was because my father was coming home and Ben didn't want to be around to face him – that's how I saw it.

There was another family tragedy about 1943 when my cousin, Ifor, who might have been a bit older than me, climbed up on the roof of the shed and fell into the pigswill my uncle was boiling up. He was badly scalded and died of shock a week later.

About this time I changed schools. I had been going to Llansamlet but changed to St Thomas's School. I was a lot happier there. I started off at Standard Five at about 12 and finished at Standard Seven at 14. When we returned to Swansea I went to Saint Thomas's school, situated on the left bank of the River Towy, just on the edge of Swansea Town. The school stands in the suburb of Saint Thomas: a tall building of brick with many windows. The suburb is a very hilly one, that may at one time been a part of Kilvey Hill, which rises behind it. The school was on two levels, to fit in with this terrain. The playground was on the lower level, at the front of the school that faces the town. There was a stairway at each end of the school, leading upwards from the playground to the classrooms at the second level.

The hard surface of the playground served as a football pitch, with games played with small rubber balls or sometimes a tennis ball. These games were very rough affairs, leading to lots of broken skin and torn clothing. This applied especially to me, usually playing as goalkeeper. I would leap in the air: I would kick away certain goals: I would run out of goal to snatch the ball from my opponent's feet: I would dive across and onto the stone and tar playground. I gained the nickname of Tiger Komich, after the Russian goalkeeper who was touring Britain with the Moscow Dynamos around that time. He was a fantastic goalie, catching the imagination of the British public with his unbelievable saves. I have heard he eventually died of a broken neck.

I was given a trial as goalkeeper for the school team but the afternoon was a disaster. I did not have the same competence with the larger ball, letting in several simple goals. Away from the playground and the smaller ball, I found myself in an alien environment. I never did wear the goalkeeper's jersey for Saint Thomas's school. I also seemed to lose much of my playground skills after that trial too and lost confidence in myself. I did however, on just one occasion, wear the school colours for the rugby team. To be honest, it was the starting up of the team in rugby, with an open invitation to anyone who fancied playing. It was a game when everyone tried to get hold of the ball, regardless of the team positions. I was unable to get near to the ball for the match, as swarms of boys surrounded the one with the ball, going from one end of the field to the other without any result.

I tagged along, but never touched leather. If I had stayed in bed that Saturday morning, I would not have been missed.

Listening to Harry Seacombe reading his autobiography on tape, I discovered teachers still at Saint Thomas's had taught Harry, a local boy, when I attended there, even although I followed some ten years after the famous Goon. One of these teachers he mentioned, a Mr. Caufield, was rumoured to have a steel plate in his head, a legacy of the First World War. He was a fine teacher, but capable of losing his rag at times, when he would go red in the face. I think all of us boys were afraid to push him too far, perhaps expecting him to go completely mad because of that steel inside him. It never happened of course, but young boys around twelve get lots of strange ideas.

Mr Caulfield taught Standard 5. Mr Ward taught Standard 6. He was a horrible teacher. His face was face full of acne scars, but even worse, he was a very strict disciplinarian, liberal with his cane. If he came into the room and saw you talking he'd cane you. A caning would leave you with a smarting hand. Then there was 'Daddy' Allen in Standard 7. He was an extrovert, a very funny man who didn't use the cane very much. He used to get boys to clean his bike.

I didn't sit the 'Eleven plus' examination. I had lost a lot of schooling through mitching and was not allowed to sit the exam. The examination was not compulsory. They would pluck out boys whom they thought might pass and groom them for success. I didn't think this was fair but that was how it was. I think that every child should have had a chance to attempt it. As it was, children who might have done well were denied a chance. Perhaps I would have done all right though. I never had a head for figures but was good in everything else but maths. At 14 I got my Leaving Card and it read 'Position in class – fourth' which was not bad. I had done pretty well in English, history, spelling and geography. (I kept that card for fifty years. It became dirtier and dirtier.)

I was quite good in art too and later in life would find great satisfaction in painting. Then, I drew comics for other kids. In those days bus conductors had a machine that would produce tickets from rolls of blank paper. I would ask my mother for spare rolls and would draw comics on them to give to other kids. (Paper was scarce in the war – once I got hold of a library book and ripped out blank pages to draw on.) The comics I drew came from the comics we read, especially the *Beano* and the *Dandy*, published in alternate weeks, at 2d a copy with covers always in full colour. We also read *Film Fun*, *Radio Fun* and *Knockout*. I loved my comics because there was art in them. Art teachers would denigrate it saying it was just technical skill but I thought that there was a lot of art in them.

Our family circumstances remained unsettled. I lived with Auntie Alice, a widow twenty years older than my father. She was very strict but she looked after us well. She made us go to chapel three times on a Sunday, putting a penny in the collection plate each time. One day I woke up to hear my father and realised he was in my room. He had fought in North Africa, Sicily and Italy but had at last got compassionate leave and a posting to Swansea to be near his children.

Ben and mother came back to Swansea and she tried to contact us children. She knocked at our front door but I didn't want to see her. She always said that when they got to Birkenhead she was taken ill and that's why she couldn't come back, but I don't believe that to be true. She didn't let the authorities know that she couldn't return – I think that they intended to leave us.

Father was 'demobbed' – demobilised – in January 1946. As a returned soldier with three children he was given priority by Swansea Corporation and given a Corporation house next door to the house we'd lived in before, in the same row where everyone knew about our past. It wasn't so much what they said but we felt their attitude made us feel inferior. Our mother had had a baby while my father had been away at the war and had run away and left us. In Swansea seventy years ago that was a lot to live down. Eventually my parents got a divorce.

Father went back to Dufferin Steelworks where he met Hilda, who was 28. She wasn't a very intelligent woman. (For example, she couldn't tell the time – she would say to herself, 'Big hand on the two, small hand on the five'.) When it was thundering she had to hide under the cupboard under the stairs. I don't know if my father married her in desperation. He had three children to care for. People didn't explain these things to children. We lived with the consequences of the divorce. When he went off to war we had furniture bought on time payments, which it seems my mother either had kept or sold. Father was still obliged to pay for the furniture he didn't own. But despite this pressure, they got on well enough. I know father could be hot-headed (as the story of my christening shows) but with Hilda he never shouted or argued.

Hilda and Father had a baby, Brian, but he was a 'blue baby' and died at 6 months – the first and last dead body I've ever seen. Then they had another boy, Jeffrey and another called Dennis who was what they used to call 'backward' – not handicapped but, like his mother, very slow. Finally they had a daughter, Carol. I had not heard anything of Jeffrey for over forty fifty years, but I met Carol when I went back to Wales in 1984. She had had a rough life, having been knocked about by her husband or boyfriend. We heard later that Carol had a seizure and collapsed and died of a brain haemorrhage but were unsure of the

Brinley and Hilda in a backyard at Bonymaen after his demobilisation in 1945. The contrast with the robust corporal in 1943 is apparent.

Tom's step-brothers and sister, Jeffrey, Caroline and Dennis.

truth of this. Hilda didn't ill-treat us but she obviously thought more of her own children. She was extravagant – buying bags of grapes for Dennis for example. At that time grapes were a luxury.

I left school at fourteen, at Easter 1946. My father and Hilda had seen an advert for a junior to work in an ironmonger's shop in Saint Thomas, not far from the school. This was one of two shops owned by a Mr. Evans, the other at Killay in Swansea West. I spent about two weeks with Mr. Evans at Killay to begin with and then worked at Saint Thomas thereafter. A woman, with whom I had a good relationship, managed the shop. But the job was poorly paid and I soon thought of looking for something better.

Before long, however, there was a change in the shop management. The lady left us for reasons I know not. In her place came an extremely short, rather ugly man with a large lump on his back. He was, I suppose, a cross between the Hunchback of Notre Dame and the artist Toulouse-Lautrec in his appearance. It seemed that he knew much about the business of ironmongery, having been with a large firm for many years. It turned out that way. He was very much the expert in ironmongery matters. Watching him talking to a customer, he was so animated about the subject matter; it was easy to forget his ugly features, the thick, heavy glasses and the large hands he used to demonstrate with. His personality was so overpowering it masked his imperfections. He had a lot more drive than the outgoing manager, apart from the new broom sweeps clean angle. He was heavily infected with the ironmongery bug: it seemed to consume him. I needed to be more on my toes now but it created more interest in the work for me. Trade bucked up because of our new manager's push and his knowledge of ironmongery.

I could not ignore the poor wages (a pound a week and I had to pay my own bus fares), however, so kept my ears open about something better. It eventually came when I heard there were vacancies at Aeron Thomas and Son, wood manufacturers at Pentrechwyth, within walking distance of home. I would be required to assist the machinist by taking away cut wood to load on a pallet. So I moved on with some regret. The work was busy but not hard. It was fairly clean work apart from the fine dust that pervaded the air from the cutting of wood. A strong smell of timber was always around but it was not unpleasant. In fact, the smell of wood and wood shavings still gives me a pleasant feeling of nostalgia.

Stacking and shifting wood was pretty dull and soon I heard that they were taking boys on at Richard Thomas & Baldwin's foundry (the Baldwin was said to be related to the former Prime Minister Stanley Baldwin). This was piece work, shovelling sand to make up so many moulds a day. We boys would shovel the fine sand up to the moulders, who would ram the sand hard to make the mould. It could be heavy work for youngsters but there was a lot of skylarking to make things entertaining. Some days we finished at 11; on other days we would knock off at 3 – hold-ups in supply of sand (a matter of luck) and on some days if all went well finished early.

I was living at home, paying rent, though my sisters and I did not get on very well with Hilda. In the evenings we listened to the wireless. Of course I was interested in meeting girls but respectable people kept their daughters on a tight rein. The only time I really met girls was at dances, at the Kilvey Hall in St Thomas on Saturday night. Entry cost two shillings, at a time when I was only making a pound – twenty shillings – a week. We danced the foxtrot, the quick step, the tango and the flirtation barn dance – my elder sister Barbara would teach me in the kitchen. The flirtation barn dance involved passing on to other partners: a lot of flirting went on. I went to dances with mates. No drink was allowed in the hall, but we went to the pub across road where I got drunk for the first time in life on a couple of pints of cider. Back in the hall I did an imitation of Al Jolson – the film *The Jolson Story* was popular at the time.

This was the heyday of the pictures. We went to the Plaza, the Carlton, the Castle, the Rialto, the Elysium or the Albert Hall. Programs usually lasted a week, changing each Monday. For a shilling you could see a couple of features, plus newsreels and cartoons. I went as often as I could. You were able to smoke in the cinema (I smoked occasionally but didn't have the money to become seriously addicted) and could buy ice creams from a girl with a tray. At the interval in some theatres a theatre organ would entertain the audience – the Plaza had an underground organ that would emerge from the stage.

We sometimes went to variety shows, such as at the Empire Theatre in cheap 9-penny seats, on benches way up in 'the gods'. If we took girls to the cinema or the theatre we would pay for more expensive seats, as much as 2/3 or even 3/6. Big names appeared at the Empire – the comedian Max Wall, the xylophone player Teddy Brown, and the singer Alan Jones. Saturday night was the big night at the Empire with queues on the pavement outside waiting for the last house.

I also went to football whenever I had the chance, following Swansea Football Club. They played in an all-white strip and were known as 'the Swans'. I saw Trevor Ford, centre-forward for Wales, the greatest centre forward Wales ever produced, who scored 41 goals in one season.

All this changed when I was seventeen when I joined the army.

3

Catterick days

One day there came a bombshell: all of us boys were to be laid off. By this time I had turned seventeen. As National Service was still in force, I would be eligible for call-up when I turned eighteen. I decided to become a regular soldier rather than wait around six months to be called up.

My father and I went into the recruiting office in Swansea where we met a very smart sergeant, complete with a red sash and I said 'I've come to join up'. My father and I sat down and talked with the sergeant. I told him that I wanted to join the Royal Armoured Corps (although my father had been in the Pioneer Corps he'd been attached to a tank unit in North Africa). This was purely a romantic notion, with no real thought on the subject. Maybe I had watched too many stirring war films. He gave me an educational test in which I immediately ran up against my old bugbear, maths. He passed me but I don't think that my marks were good enough for the Royal Armoured Corps. This seemed to cast a shadow over my career with the Royal Armoured Corps. I soon found that I was out of my depth, or that was the way I felt about it.

I took the oath to the King, joining up for five years with the colours and seven in the reserve. I was ordered to report to Catterick in Yorkshire, supplied with a rail warrant, then wished good luck by the recruiting sergeant. I was to do my basic training with the 17th/21st Lancers. The Royal Armoured Corps still retained the old names of the cavalry regiments. The motto of the Lancers, I learned, being 'Death or Glory', with a cap badge of skull and crossbones. This was my first time away from home and I had to travel half-way across the country. It was September 1949 and I was exactly seventeen and a half.

It was a long journey from South Wales to Yorkshire. I journeyed overnight, reaching the camp in the early morning at breakfast time. I was taken to the cookhouse where I was given a feed that restored my flagging spirits somewhat. From that time on I was under a Welsh sergeant who seemed to take an instant dislike to me. He never let a chance pass to ridicule me in front of the others training with me. It was difficult for me to understand. I did not expect special treatment from him because of our mutual nationality but he seemed to go out of his way to taunt me. If I was having difficulty with the drill, his approach

Tom aged 18, with a leek attached to his beret on
St David's Day, Chester 1951.

simply did nothing to help things. I have wondered over the years if the man had a complex on being Welsh. I have heard of such people, feeling a dislike of their roots and anyone to remind them of them. Perhaps I was so bad on the parade ground he was ashamed? It is something I can only guess about, on events so long ago. I can remember how the situation gradually wore away my confidence, piece by piece.

I was then ordered to join the 14th/20th Hussars, stationed a small distance away. I left behind the awful sergeant, but not all my problems. I found it difficult to fit in with these Englishmen. There was one from Ulster, with whom I had some connection. He had joined up as a regular, with a plan to lose himself over the border in the Irish Free State if things didn't go his way. Later I heard he had gone without a trace so I suppose he had followed up his plan. I never heard any more about him. He had obviously been as despondent and disillusioned as I was. There were few romantic notions left in me by this time. One Englishman I did have a friendship with was a chap called Russell. His first name now escapes me.

No 37 Serial Troop 5 ¾yeo Kings Hussars Tp Off' ²/Lt Lewis Tp Sgt Pemberton Inst'/cpl Millage

The troop of the 14th/20th Hussars, with which Tom briefly served: Trooper Stevens is fourth from right in back row.

What I do remember about him was his extremely red face. He always appeared as though he had just come in from a ten-mile run, or perhaps having gone several rounds in boxing. He seemed very healthy and having spent much time in the open air.

Eventually, I learned I was to be posted to Germany, with Russell going to Hong Kong. To prove that I had a lot yet to know about the Army, I made the request to go with Russell to the Far East. It was just a matter of friendship, nothing more. Maybe the Army saw the shadow of homosexuality or did not approve of close friendships so I found my request turned down. Russell went off to Hong Kong whereas I was packed off to a dead end posting at Aldershot. We had had the most innocent of friendships but I broke a cardinal rule in asking to stay with him. Off I went then to Mons Officer Cadet School where I would serve out my penance doing some menial job or other. Within a short time I found myself a regular at the Sergeants' Mess doing the washing up.

Before I move on though, I would like to relate a small story of a guard detail I did before leaving Catterick. The night was very dark and very cold. The fellow I was relieving at one point during the night, passed on a tip about a boiler room that was warm and cosy. I could not bring myself to stay there for too long, feeling a mixture of guilt and fear of being caught there by the guard corporal. I would patrol around in a wind that tried its best to cut me in half and then duck into the boiler room to thaw out somewhat. When I got too comfortable, it was time to move out into the elements once again. What a great feeling it was to enjoy the warmth after a spell outside! The long Yorkshire night was made much easier because of that boiler room.

Towards the end of the night and the guard, the corporal told me to go with him to the ATS barracks (the Auxiliary Territorial Service – the women's army corps). He said that a peeping tom had been reported around the place so we should take a look around to try and catch him in the act. We were able to see several women getting dressed through the blinds covering the window. It was all about shape and shadow only but it offers a certain stimulation to a seventeen year old. There was no sign of the peeping tom, so after a bit of a floorshow, the corporal said we should leave. It was only later that I worked out who was the peeping tom. The corporal had obviously done that particular guard before, knowing about the women putting on a show. The peeping tom bit was just an excuse to get a good eyeful, using me as a defence should we be caught out. The corporal would just say we were looking for this imaginary prowler. I can't say I was all that upset about being used that way, however! It is strange the women were not aware of shapes showing through the blinds. Perhaps they did know, enjoying a little teasing themselves!

It was a very drab life washing up at the Sergeants' Mess at Aldershot. There was a little entertainment here and there, however. I remember one bloke on the washing up detail who had a particular gripe about one of the sergeants. One lunch-time, he was one of those carrying plates of food along a corridor to a serving hatch, where the plates were taken over by white-coated waiters then distributed to the tables. The man did some disgusting things with one meal in the corridor, one being to spit into the food, another to do interesting things with his penis. He then passed the lunch through to a waiter at the serving hatch, when the food was then given to the poor unfortunate sergeant who probably enjoyed what was put before him. Revenge is sweet, but that was a pretty vile thing to do, I thought.

I cannot recall how it came about but it happened I was rescued from dirty pots and pans, to become a clerk in the camp office. I had a very soft job at the office where leave passes and train warrants were organised and written out. I worked under the supervision of a corporal with a very apt name. Corporal Salmon had the misfortune actually to look like a fish. He had eyes that were very fish-like, with a mouth to match. He was a very nice fellow to work with, so I really had fallen into a bed of roses. One time I had the very enjoyable task of writing out my own leave pass and rail warrant. These did not become valid until an officer signed them of course.

As time passed, I became bored with office work. When I heard the Royal Welch Fusiliers would shortly be going to Jamaica, I decided to seek a transfer to them. It sounded a much better deal than sitting in an office all day. I sat down to write out my request to the Commanding Officer, saying among other things that I was Welsh, with a wish to see overseas service. I did not really expect the request to be granted but I thought it worth a shot. I thought the one thing in my favour was the fact of being Welsh. I hoped it would be enough to swing things my way.

In due course I was notified to appear on Commanding Officer's Orders to know if I had permission to join the Royal Welch Fusiliers. The Regimental Sergeant Major taking charge of things that morning had a certain fame in the British Army. He was RSM Ronald Brittain of the Guards, deemed to have the loudest voice in the army. The man was stout but tall, so carried himself well. The cadets who aspired to the King's Commission feared him. His loud voice would tell them how idle they were, among other abuse, but always ending with the word sir or sirs. It was somewhere in this period the RSM had a role, playing himself in a film of the Second World War. It was a film about the Welsh Guards called *They Were Not Divided*. This then was the terror that called me to attention outside the Commanding Officer's office that morning. I am sure the windows rattled as that great booming voice roared his command. It was an effort to stop my legs having a bit of a rattle of their own.

All went very well. I was granted the transfer, to join the Royal Welch Fusiliers after a leave at Christmas, which was very near. I was to report to Brecon Training Camp to join up with men already in training there. Before I knew it, I was outside the office, being ordered to fall out by the giant guardsman. I felt as if I had won a large sum of money. Soon I would be out of the Royal Armoured Corps, with me just as glad to be out of it as they probably were to see me go. We had not got along terribly well.

I had one romantic dalliance at Aldershot. The girl was from nearby Woking, just a short rail journey away. I went to her home at times and there was even talk of her coming to Wales with me for a visit. It all came to nothing though, with everything ending before I got my transfer.

I went home for seven days' leave at Christmas. These days went by on wings, to see me preparing to set off for Brecon and the Fusiliers' depot. My father came with me to catch the bus at Swansea on a Sunday night. I suddenly became aware I did not have my army greatcoat, which I had folded up to carry over one arm. It soon became clear that I had left it on the bus to Swansea. My father thought we should wait for the bus to come around again to where we had got off. I did not hold out much hope of seeing it again, not making a great start at my new life and new camp. The bus pulled in with the greatcoat in the arms of the conductor, who must have seen us at the bus stop. I was so pleased, to think now this was a good omen for the future. How quickly things can turn around in life.

I left Swansea in a double-decker bus for the hour and half or so it would take to Brecon. The night was very cold and miserable before it got even worse as we came into snow. The bus groaned trying to climb a hill clothed in snow and ice. All passengers got off the bus to lighten the load and push from behind. Eventually the bus made it to the top of the hill, where we all got in again. From then on it was a clear run to Brecon.

There didn't seem a great deal of life going on in what to me seemed a small market town, typical of rural Wales. I did see the lights of a public house, to which I made my way to buy a packet of cigarettes. The first person I saw as I entered was a chap called Williams, someone from the same part of town where I came from. I did not know him terribly well – he was a little older than me – but we recognised each other at once. I saw he was wearing the black flash and shoulder patch of the Royal Welch Fusiliers. I believe I may have shared a beer with him as I asked questions such as the way to the camp. He said he was going back there himself, with me welcome to tag along with him. As we walked along in the darkness, he told me he had been in the Welsh Guards originally. I am unable to remember the facts of his transfer, but I suspect he had been naughty in one way or another. He was a bit of a character but good company when reasonably sober. I would later discover him to play the best bugle in the battalion.

I found myself back in basic training again, joining men about half way through theirs. One cold morning I was slow to respond to a sergeant coming around telling us to get out of bed. The result was I finished up with three days confined to barracks. Once more I found myself amongst dirty pots and pans and dishes. In those three days I met up with a Fusilier Griffiths, who was also on jankers. It was a brief friendship, but I did not forget the chap. Much later he was sent home from Jamaica, suffering badly with asthma. The poor chap died on the commercial ship he had been despatched on and was then buried at sea. It was such a young age to leave this life behind.

I got on with my life in the infantry without any more real mishaps, finding bleak Brecon just about as cold as Yorkshire. Then I went on embarkation leave, for what I think was twenty-one days. I teamed up with a local boy called John Davies who was also on RAF embarkation leave for Singapore for the same period as me. We spent our time around and about Swansea, visiting a variety of public houses and dance halls. I got to know a girl called Vera, from Ystalyfera, which by the nature of things was a very brief romance. Still, we promised to write to each other, which we did for some time. Eventually all the fun and games came to an end with John and I also promising to keep in touch by letter.

The First Battalion of the Royal Welch Fusiliers was to return to Chester from Germany to prepare for the tour of the West Indies. I and many of the chaps I had been with at Brecon, joined up with them there. Here we were issued with tropical kit and attended lectures and films on the dangers of VD. I found Chester a much

Tom's locker by his bed, with a photograph of Vera, a woman from Ystalyfera, near Swansea, to whom he wrote for a while.

more interesting place than tiny Brecon. There were lots of pubs and cinemas and good eating-places. We did our best to enjoy the town, with the date of sailing fixed for March 1951. I was full of expectation of the three years that lay ahead. Why did I not have the foresight to think of keeping a journal?

Before sailing we celebrated Saint David's Day on the first of March, the first time I had done so in a Welsh regiment. The youngest soldier in the battalion was expected to devour a small leek, standing on a table after the special dinner provided that day, served to the men by officers. He ate the leek to a drum roll, with men of the band dressed in the scarlet uniforms of a previous time. On this Saint David's Day I had a studio photograph taken, looking too young to be a soldier, with a leek pinned on my beret near the regimental badge. I would celebrate my nineteenth birthday on the twenty-fifth day of that same month of March. By then, though, I would be on my way to Jamaica.

4

Newcastle days

I had not seen a naked woman before and when I did there were two of them. Two tall, golden-coloured Jamaicans asked to use the shower in our toilet block. A group of us watched enthralled as they lathered long, shapely limbs; the women letting the water caress their bodies with a sensuous embrace, as if the water washed away more than grime and sweat of the day. As they soaped themselves, we gathered they had come up from Kingston. The two women were, I could see, well into their twenties (older than many of us) and possessed the hardened look of feral animals. But their bodies remained firm and supple, with large breasts that wobbled about as they jumped around in the showers. For all of their sexual attraction, the fear of VD was strong in my mind, at least in those very early days and most of us probably felt the same. These two temptresses went off somewhere and I never saw them again. Their intentions remained unclear, but they were probably hoping to find a bed, with food or money thrown in, in one of the barrack rooms, in exchange for sex of course. If anyone took up the offer I never knew.

Our company had been chosen to spend the first tour of duty at Newcastle. The camp was ideal for training, away from the heat and bustle of Kingston. The cool air and the mountain's lush vegetation, coupled with natural tracks winding around the camp, made Newcastle the perfect spot for training courses known as 'cadres'. The main course was for the development of NCOs, supported by a company stationed there to carry out the normal camp duties which would also include being the enemy to the aspiring NCOs. Although our military duties were reasonably demanding, our free time left us with little to do and few places to go in such a forlorn place. The camp had a church hall that served as a cinema, with films brought up from Kingston. Then there was a NAAFI* where soldiers were able to purchase little luxuries and splurge on pay night, with a plate of egg and chips. But this just about covered the social life of the troops. There was neither library nor reading room, unlike at Kingston. Many men spent too much time drinking at the NAAFI, or in the barracks, in an effort to kill the nights of

---

* 'Navy, Army and Air Force Institute' – the organisation that provided canteens and shops to the forces.

Greetings from Jamaica. B. W. I.

Newcastle

A postcard of Newcastle camp, suggesting how it gave troops respite from the heat of the coastal plain around Kingston.

boredom. It has occurred to me since that we might have bought a radio collectively: why we did not remains a mystery.

At the heart of the camp was the barrack square. Near the square there was a wall bearing badges in relief of the different regiments that had been there over the years. On the slopes running down from the square were the half-dozen barrack blocks in which we lived, hugging the mountainside.

I became a camp policeman purely on the strength of being a regular soldier. (Camp policemen were selected from regular soldiers rather than National Servicemen.) There was no special uniform, just a black armband with the letters CP in green, standing for 'Camp Police'. The job was not a matter of brawn (I was not built for it anyway), but more a matter of being observant around the camp, which virtually looked after itself; and going around Newcastle, in pairs usually, with a time clock on a shoulder strap. At certain parts of the route, we were required to place a key (provided there) in the clock, which would record our time of being there. This was to provide evidence the next day to our superiors of being alert and patrolling our designated journey. Well, at least it showed we passed that way, if nothing else.

The camp was unenclosed, explaining why the Jamaican women were able to turn up in our barrack-room. Rising upward from the square were the church hall and NAAFI and several houses scattered around, used as married quarters. An extremely old wooden building, just in front of the church hall served as our post office, with an elderly Jamaican woman doing the honours as postmistress. It was here we posted our letters and parcels to the UK. Our own mail was brought up from Kingston in the daily ration truck and handed out to us by an NCO.

The NAAFI was a popular place, of course, the outlet where we purchased our cigarettes and beer. The Jamaican brands of smokes, known as Four Aces and Royal Blend, were very good in flavour and popular. If my memory serves correctly, British brands such as Players were available at a price, but the Jamaican brands suited most men. The Jamaican popular bottled beer, Red Stripe, was served ice cold and most had no quarrel with the taste there either. The church hall was used as a cinema once a week and was always well attended. There was only one projector, so there would be an enforced break between reels. I have strong memories of watching Larry Parks in the sequel to *The Jolson Story*, the great follow-up *Jolson Sings Again*, in this manner. Seeing this film advertised (for TV) usually evoke thoughts of that night in Newcastle, with the long intervals between the Jolson memories. In today's environment, watching commercial television, it is the normal state of affairs: a piece of the action between the advertisements.

Further up the mountain, beyond the buildings, was the ground used for training purposes: plenty of thick foliage, through which many dirt tracks wound their way up and over the top of our mountain. This part of Newcastle was sub-tropical and was where I first made contact with a machete, used by us to cut through the undergrowth. During the wet season the ground became a quagmire and almost impossible to negotiate. No doubt in times previous, many snakes would have passed through that country but they had been wiped out through the introduction to Jamaica of the mongoose. They had succeeded in this endeavour, only to create another problem: the overrunning of the mongoose!

Jamaican women coming to the camp from the surrounding dwellings, would offer a washing and ironing service at a most reasonable price. These 'dhobi' women, as we called them (the term dhobi was a throwback to the days of the Raj in India), were nearly always barefoot and dressed with a head covering of material wrapped in a turban. This helped, no doubt, in the basket-carrying on the crown of their heads, containing the laundry. Sometimes a great deal of bargaining would transpire over the washing and a 'dhobi' woman might express her anger at the attempted exploitation by calling the offender a 'Ras.'

This term of 'Ras' referred to the Jamaican cult of Rastafarianism; believing in black supremacy, with a 'back-to-Africa' agenda. The name followed from 'ras

Tafari', which Emperor Haile Selassie of Ethiopia had used when crowned in 1930. The cult followers considered the still-living Emperor a god. The story in those times had the Rastafaris living in the Cockpit Country, in the island's interior, where ordinary folks feared to tread, as the Rastas had the reputation as wild, drug-taking bad men. These rebels wore their hair long, usually with a beard and smoked marijuana; this was long before the hippies of the 'sixties.

Although there was a growing movement towards independence for Jamaica, it was on a political level rather than in any form of terrorist organisation. We found most Jamaican people to be decent, law abiding citizens, in spite of the grinding poverty which many endured. Considering we were in reality an occupying army, they responded to us with a surprisingly positive attitude. The Jamaicans had their own Jamaica Regiment, but this force came under the wing of the British commander of Caribbean Forces, which denied it being an independent military arm. The headquarters of this regiment was at Kingston, at a camp other than our battalion's station of Up Park camp; but all forces worked closely with the other and with the Jamaica Regiment operating on the same military lines as the British Army and, soon forged a solid bond with the Royal Welch Fusiliers. Curiously, I never saw any of them actually carrying arms. Whether this was a prudent precaution I don't know. The Jamaicans also had women soldiers.

As I began to find my feet in this new land, I began searching out the background history of Jamaica and the Caribbean. The island was about 130 kilometres south of Cuba, still in those days under the rule of the dictator Batista. Soon a young lawyer called Fidel Castro would bring about a revolution to sweep this corrupt regime from power and install himself as dictator. This would give America much to think about.

Jamaica is an island of much natural beauty, consisting of an elevated plain bisected by the Blue Mountains running east to west. Columbus was the credited discoverer of Jamaica, on his second voyage in 1494. It remained under Spanish domination until Britain took the island from them in 1655. Many of the Spanish fled into the interior and with their followers, gave the authorities a great deal of problems in the years to come. Kingston, a city at the edge of the sparkling Caribbean, replaced the former capital of Spanish Town situated several kilometres inland.

The name of Jamaica comes from the aboriginal word, Xaymaca (land of wood and water). The original inhabitants of the island: the Arawaks who had inhabited Jamaica for some five hundred years before the Spanish, came originally from South America. When the Spanish invaders set foot on the island the natives made rude noises and pulled strange faces in an effort to scare away the new arrivals. They soon capitulated to the Spanish invasion on seeing the heavily armed sailors and their aggressive dogs. Jamaica did not at first come under the Spanish crown, as had many of the discoveries of the explorer. Instead, it became the personal property of the Columbus family. At the beginning of Spanish settlement, the Spaniards settled at St. Ann's Bay on the north coast, which they knew as Sevilla Nueva. Later, they moved to the other side of the island which began the settling of Spanish Town, known by them as Villa de la Vega.

The Spaniards were hungry for gold and Jamaica proved to be a land rich in beauty but poor in the yellow metal so prized by the invaders. They ruled with an iron fist and this treatment, together with the introduction of European diseases, gradually decimated the Indian population. The original inhabitants were eventually exterminated. The Spanish occupiers then began to introduce African slaves to perform the mundane tasks not relished by the oppressors. These slaves developed the island for their later British masters, who introduced sugar plantations and became rich men.

Facts such as these began to make themselves known to me as I settled in to my new life in the Blue Mountains. Hitherto I knew Jamaica only as a pirate stronghold in the days of Henry Morgan but had little other knowledge. Now, I walked the hills, meeting people like the elderly American couple on vacation who came to Newcastle for a look, staying to chat with a crowd of us and having snapshots taken at the start of the steps leading down to the barracks. I remember them as very nice people.

Things for me changed dramatically one night when I drank too much rum. I had little tolerance for this potent drink in those early days and after many tots of rum, very little common sense remained in a befuddled mind. In the barrack room where several of us were drinking, celebrating nothing in particular, an argument broke out during which I began arguing with Corporal James in an apparently aggressive manner. It was not me talking, but Captain Morgan Jamaican rum. After this, everything blacked out for me until waking up in the guardhouse next morning. This was the same guardhouse from which I had operated as a camp policeman. Later that morning I appeared before Major Bosanquet, our company commander, charged with speaking to Corporal James in a threatening manner and being drunk and disorderly. Since I could remember very little of these events, there was not a lot I could say in my defence. Major Bosanquet was really a good officer but he had little choice other than sentence me to seven days in the guardroom. In a stern, yet fatherly way, he reminded me of my position as policeman and regular soldier which should set an example to the National Servicemen; before informing me I would not miss the company training which was about to commence. I was to serve my sentence but was allowed to join in the day's training before being escorted back to my cell. This was an abrupt turn around in my life: from policeman to prisoner at the same jail, in a very short space of time. As yet no NCO cadres had commenced at the Newcastle camp and the period of training for 'C' Company was probably to remind us we were still in the army. Life had suddenly turned on its head.

I was escorted to my cell, marching at quick time, with the night guard to keep me company. After a long night I was marched to the company cookhouse for my breakfast and then returned to the guardroom to prepare myself for the day of training. Marching on the square to team up with my fellow trainees was not a pleasant experience. They stood by the high wire fence at the barracks side of the square, smoking and joking before we were called on parade. I felt a prime idiot. The camp policeman, previously a mate, who had escorted me to breakfast and also to training, now returned to the guardroom to carry on his duties; leaving me to the sniggers of the assembled troops and the tender mercy of Sergeant Trimble, the bulky Englishman with a permanently foul disposition. I had the feeling, as the first morning wore on, I was being singled out by the good sergeant for special treatment, perhaps as a part of my punishment. Being ordered to strip down and re-assemble a Bren gun, I made rather a hash of it, allowing myself to be intimidated. Also I had little skill with my hands in those days; skill which I later developed as confidence grew. I remember being told to mend a puncture in a bicycle wheel in one military test but could not: I had never owned a bicycle. Growing up in wartime, where I lived in Swansea, the nearest I ever came to such a thing was the 'boneshaker' assembled from bicycle parts from the rubbish dump. This Frankenstein of the road had no tyres or seat and clanked and shook vigorously as I rode along the main street past my home. There was no need of a puncture outfit.

Sergeant Trimble, in a voice heavily laced with sarcasm, asked if I had a problem; to which I stupidly told him I was not particularly mechanically minded. This seemed to set off a bomb inside him, as he began to almost melt with anger from the sheer forces within. I do not recall the retaliation from the sergeant that morning, although I am certain it would not have been good, but one thing I do remember is making an enemy that day. Things had reached rock bottom. The Bren gun had a tendency to jam: hence the ability to take the gun apart was vital. It is open to question however, on the best method of instruction: the surly aggressive approach (that is, Sergeant Trimble), or a more restrained, calm, helpful attitude. Respect can lead to respect in turn, even in the army.

The day's training drew to an end and, as the remainder clambered down the stone steps to their barracks, I was told to march myself off to the cell that awaited me. An NCO escorted me, marching smartly two or three paces behind me, before handing me over to the resident policeman at the guardhouse.

The days passed as they always do and soon the training and cell confinement ended at a simultaneously, when I returned to barrack room living, but not to my former police duties. I now became a member of the general duties mob, carrying out tasks of little significance but now eligible for night guard duty, from which I had previously been exempt.

I found the very small military graveyard at Newcastle a poignant place. Reading the weatherworn headstones, it became obvious how the scourge of Yellow Fever had made soldiering in the West Indies a risky business. I wondered how different life for the Newcastle garrison would have been those many years past, with their heavy uniforms, poor mail service, no cinema or radio, with all the health problems and poor pay. The surrounding hills, I thought, would have been very much the same as when these men had performed their duties in centuries gone; and they had slept on in the small graveyard, through many chilly Newcastle nights and the singing of the bullfrogs before the warm sun moved over the mountains, in their resting place so far from Britain. The cemetery was situated on the other side of the dirt and rock roadway running down the valley, passing by the last of the barrack rooms that hugged the mountain. Near the entrance was the lane, branching away from the road, which led the way, past the undergrowth, to the shooting range and beyond that the sports field, a leveled piece of ground at the bottom of the valley. The cemetery was overgrown with long grasses, with the headstones leaning at odd angles: one or two completely out of the ground. I often visited this place, reading of the early deaths of many of the occupants.

In our barrack room and in most others the central part of the room was the long table and wooden chairs positioned between the beds lined up against the walls. It was the gaming room (for cards), the library (where books were read and letters written) and also served as the bar where we drank our beer and guzzled our rum. The table was the axis of our lives, around which most things revolved after the day's duties. In true army style, our blankets and sheets were folded to the same length and width each morning and placed at the head of the bed for possible inspection. Every man had his own steel locker next to his bed, always left unlocked, to allow inspection by an NCO or officer. Usually a soldier was selected to act as the room orderly for the day. His job was the care and supervision of the barracks until the residents finished their duties for the day. Regulations were very relaxed on the mountain in comparison to battalion headquarters at Kingston. Although there was an official time for 'lights out' (I think it was 10 p.m.), it was not strictly enforced. Even the relationships between NCOs and other ranks were more relaxed, as a general rule.

There were many days when cloud hung over the mountain hiding the sun, days also of cool greyness and rain. The nights could be on the cool side, but good for a night's sleep. There was a sense of family in the camp, being just a company; we all knew each other closely. There seemed a closer bond with each other on the mountain. I was to discover that life at Kingston would be different.

Then suddenly the cadres started to happen, which changed things somewhat, but did not entirely kill the comradeship of 'C' Company. The men taking part in the cadres, NCOs from Kingston, were billeted together and usually kept their own company. The church hall had a bigger audience for film nights and it was harder to get served at the NAAFI but life did not change drastically. Besides, the cadres, lasting for some six weeks, did not go on all the time, with intervals of weeks between each one.

Our company was allocated the task of being the 'enemy' for the battalion 'Internal Security Scheme'. This order dictated that we were not allowed to shave and required us to parade daily as scruffily as we could make ourselves. Although

'A view that was to become so much part of our lives': Kingston seen from
Newcastle at night.

the local population really posed no threat to us, it was necessary for all troops to have training on riot and crowd control experience. Daily on the square we shouted wildly, brandishing sticks in simulated anger dressed in civilian clothes. The local Jamaicans, passing by, must have thought we had been out in the sun too long. In the end I did not finish this training program, because I was ordered to Kingston before it ended. There I was to take part in an Educational centre in company with Fusilier Alexander, an Englishman from Birmingham, also of 'C' Company. We were both to be attached to Support Company during the period of the course and we would be away from Newcastle for several weeks. There was one by-product of this excursion: we would get our first opportunity to visit the fleshpots of the capital. We packed our kit bags and prepared to leave the mountain retreat aboard the ration truck on its journey to Kingston.

Looking out on the winding road as we worked our way down the mountain, I felt anxious about the course ahead. I had always had a difficulty with maths, part of the problem being much missed schooling during the war and had not really put them to any practical use since leaving school at fourteen. I hoped I would be able to find the time and ability to swot enough to scrape through. Soon Newcastle became an assortment of buildings hugging the mountain far above us. We hit the plain, with the vehicle now hopping along in top gear, making its way to Up Park camp. It was early into a Saturday afternoon and I wondered if it would be possible to leave camp that evening and also, did I want to? First things first, I decided; the priority was to be settled in first, making certain of a bed for the night.

5

Kingston and a wind

Arriving at Support Company headquarters we made ourselves known and were taken to the stores to be supplied with bedding. Being Saturday, the storeman had to be located by the duty sergeant who had taken Alexander and I under his wing. From the stores, carrying our sheets and blankets, we were directed to a barrack room where we would join members of Support Company and be part of that small world until the end of our stay in Kingston.

The hustle-bustle of the Headquarters seemed alien after our 'comfortable' existence up on the mountain. It took several days to start swimming in the new pool and become a part of Support Co., if only temporarily. Alex, as I came to know him, and I began our studies on the Monday after our arrival. We did this at the Education Centre, under the jurisdiction of an Education Corps sergeant. As I had feared, the maths was going to be a problem for me but I tried to keep optimistic about the situation.

I found Alex a hard man to know. His conversation was limited to only what he found necessary to say. There seemed no passion in the man and I put it down to him being English. Nevertheless, he was very practical and, I noticed, had a good grasp of maths in class. Off duty Alex liked the grog, not being too interested in the cinema. I, too, in those times, liked a drink, but not to the exclusion of other pursuits which included my love of film. Although Alex and I did have some social outings together, we also went our own ways to do our own things. I had absorbed some lessons from the booze life-style, such as the seven days 'inside' at Newcastle and knew it could be an expensive hobby. Those who followed 'the drink' could expect to be always short of money and always on the borrow. It was not the way I chose to go.

Going to see a film at one of Kingston's cinemas initially had me waiting for the film to stop for a change of reel, as at Newcastle and it was a little while before this wore off. The cinemas were of a good standard, many of them open-aired and in those pre-television days, very well patronised. There were one or two theatres considered to be 'risky', being in a rough part of the city and mostly made up of rough neck Jamaicans; mostly young Turks full of bravado. If going to these places and sometimes it was tempting with a good film showing, it was a sound idea to go in pairs, at the very least. With the 'mainline' cinemas it was safe enough to go alone and I did so many times without a hint of trouble. The camp also provided a film show, usually once a week, using the parade ground as the theatre. At the edge of the parade ground a large screen, laced to poles stood always ready for use, while wooden chairs were usually placed in position by men on punishment. All that was required from the patrons was to turn up and pay admission. The fee was not a high one. In the event of bad weather, the cookhouse where we ate our meals was the alternative venue. The film and place of showing were advertised on the cookhouse notice board on the day of the screening and sometimes in a sudden weather change, simply by word of mouth.

The days moved into August and from about the middle of that month, reports in the press and the radio told of a hurricane moving in Jamaica's direction. On the morning of the 17th, one weather report had the hurricane entering into a dangerous stage, being centred some 160 kilometres to the south east of the eastern tip of the island. As the day progressed, phase warnings were issued, with various precautionary measures being taken. By 6p.m. almost everything that could be done had been done and it then became purely a matter of waiting for the big wind to hit. A little later than this I was at the NAAFI at Up Park camp, with everyone on the surface appearing calm and normal; an air of expectancy giving a strange feature of unreality to events. There were few of us who knew what to expect apart from a small number of old hands that had experienced a typhoon in Hong Kong. I can remember leaving the NAAFI to walk to my barracks and having this sense of unreality follow me, as I walked in an evening of such strange calmness, which was indeed the calm before the storm. At the barracks we had a supply of tinned food and fresh water stacked and stored in the room, with a radio tuned into the local Radio Jamaica bulletins giving reports and advice. At 9p.m. the Governor of the island, His Excellency, Sir Hugh Foot (brother of Michael Foot, famous left-wing firebrand of British politics) spoke on the radio; but even as he did so, trees were being uprooted in Kingston with the first gusts of Hurricane Charlie, as it was named. I remember listening to the radio, when hearing a moan, loud and long from out there in the darkness. The hurricane had announced its arrival, like a suffering animal locked in chains and struggling for its freedom.

It was approximately 10 p.m. when the 100-mile-an-hour wind struck Kingston in a fury that surprised us all, huddled in our barracks. Horizontal rain forced its way under tiles and roofs, with the noise simply overwhelming. All kinds of debris, lifted, torn away, including whole sheets of iron, thrashed around in the blinding rain and crazy wind. Tree branches sailed past the barrack room windows as though they were puny matchsticks, bouncing and flying in madness. Power lines broke free and danced crazily in the rain and wind-filled night.

The scenes of mayhem became visible in the intense darkness by the flashes of lightning turning night into day. The darkness would return, allowing the noises of the storm to continue around us in an alarming way. It was hard to know which was the more frightening: to see the wildness of the storm in the explosion of bright light or to hear it only in a darkness as black as the grave. The sheer driving sheets of rain, as heavy as rods of steel, hammered on roofs, forcing abandonment of any possible conversation beneath. In other barracks to our own, some Royal Welchmen had to resort to standing inside their steel lockers to keep dry. We were to learn later of the Officers' Mess at Newcastle, being thought of as a safe haven, was crammed with families and officers. The determined rain, forcing its way under the eaves, allowed streams of water to run along the floors, making any rest that night a contest of endurance, moving mattresses to avoid the flood.

Also at Newcastle, the NAAFI lost its roof during the night and the camp itself became isolated when the torrent of rain, in tandem with the high winds washed

Damage from Hurricane Charlie, Kingston, August 1951.

he road away in many spots. A rainfall of 17 inches, in a 12-hour period was recorded in that area. The main Newcastle and Kingston road winds around the mountain as a snake, being just a ledge of earth and rock in places. The rushing water ate through such parts of the road, driving the earth down the mountain into rivers of mud. Later I was to learn too of Major Bosanquet of Newcastle having his car washed away and he was unable to recover it for a month.

A book I read many years later told of a soldier being decapitated by a flying corrugated iron sheet. But I am certain that it was not a member of the Royal Welch Fusiliers. I can only assume it was a soldier of the Jamaica Regiment although I did not hear about it at the time.

Later that evening we lost our power. We had no light other than hurricane lamps and candles. It was not possible to turn on a radio to know exactly what was happening. It is amazing to me now when I think of it, but eventually, through all the bedlam of the storm, I actually went off into a deep slumber, broken in the course of the night by men with flashlights entering our room and shouting out to ask if we were safe. There was water in rivulets on the floor, finding its way under doors and around the windows, making things sodden. Many of us began to stir from a stupor, realising the hurricane had passed on, but not the havoc it had left in its wake. Men moved around, protecting shoes and boots from under their beds from the pools of water. Outside, the great wind had blown itself out, but an occasional gust or two in its weakened state still left echoes of the force we had witnessed. There was the sound of things still being thrown about the parade ground, near to our hut, but the intense anger of the hurricane had now gone. Rain still dripped from roofs and trees, those trees still standing. All around the camp, soldiers jabbered about the night's events, lit up cigarettes and realised they had lived through a small part of history, as far as Jamaica was concerned. We had experienced a night to remember for many years ahead.

Dawn came slowly through a washed out, tired grey sky, reluctantly facing the deaths and damage to be revealed in the hours ahead. And almost as the morning overpowered the darkness, we were suddenly ordered into battle order. We wore the standard dress worn for real action: steel helmet, small pack, pouches (for ammunition), rifle and bayonet. Rumors flew around as we hastened into our jackets, shorts, puttees and boots and raced over to the armoury to sign out our rifles. When we were issued with five rounds to each man, it became evident things were getting serious. Soon Support Company stood on parade, on a parade ground strewn with debris. Where there were depressions in the bitumen, miniature lakes of rainwater showed the violence of the night. The miserable sky, a swirling, cheerless window of heaving, dark clouds had a Monday morning back-to-work feel about it and there was a coolness now after the steamy build up the day before.

The officer standing before us gave the general story on what was happening. During the wild storm, parts of the civilian prison in the capital had collapsed and seventy male prisoners had escaped. Male prisoners had broken into the women's prison, where rape and consensual sex had taken place. Following these events, the male convicts had vanished into the night, on the run in and out of the city. Our detachment of troops had been assigned to the prison to reinforce the civilian warders, in the hoped-for recapture and return of the prisoners. We were warned of our responsibilities carrying live ammunition and not to load our weapons until ordered.

We climbed aboard the vehicles that were to take us to the prison, the usual manouvering taking place to get the spot by the open arch of the lorry, rather than the stuffy enclosure further inside, which offered little view through the tangle of men in helmets and equipment. The vehicles moved away, immediately driving into a sheet of water, sending up a spray that for a second put a brake on the trucks passing through.

Driving through the camp, we began to see some of the damage caused by Hurricane Charlie. Trees were down everywhere, uprooted with ease, thrown across the roads leading in and out of Up Park camp. Our battalion adjutant, Captain Whittaker (an excellent marksman) made the clearing of the roads his first priority. The captain, as direct as his shooting for the battalion's rifle team, knew the arteries of the city were the link to all help and relief. He acted with appropriate haste, making it possible, among other things, to proceed to the prison. Men worked to remove the fallen trees, as we drove through the camp and beyond, heading for downtown Kingston and the jail. Very few people were on the streets, where the trail of the hurricane had found out the flimsy, mostly wooden structures. Many buildings had severe damage, some piled together in a crazy mixture of walls and roof, in a hotchpotch of rubble. We were to discover later that Kingston was virtually isolated. It was difficult to get in or out of the city.

Our party was under the command of Major the Lord Wynford, an officer with only one arm, but a very experienced soldier. On arrival at the prison, our group lined up to be briefed by the Major, before marching into the jail, onto the courtyard inside, protected on all sides by the buildings of the prison. Brought to a halt, we were, at this stage, told to 'stand easy,' before being instructed to load our rifles with the clip of five rounds and to engage the safety switch (or catch). We were now able to see the warders, all Jamaicans, forming up in two, large, separate groups, facing each other. These men were armed with truncheons, which they had drawn and held close to their chests. There was an air of expectancy about the proceedings, before the first prisoner recaptured was dragged into the arena. He was made to run the gauntlet between the eager warders, anxious to vent their spleen on the unfortunate man. This they did with a vengeance, bringing their batons down in a rain of blows, causing him to cry out in a voice laced with fear. The prisoner cried out to Jesus, God, or anyone else who might help him but the blows continued until he had passed through the human archway before he was shuffled away to confinement. More prisoners were brought in; picked up all over the city. We stood, nervously watching the men being put through this tunnel of pain. Many tried to protect their heads by raising their arms. This did them little good, as the warders then aimed for the prisoners' private parts, causing them to scream out in agony as the sticks laid into their testicles. All the while, our party had stood in an alert state as a back-up to the prison custodians, who certainly took full advantage. Much later, an officer of the Royal Welch Fusiliers, not Lord Wynford, wrote to the *Daily Gleaner*, Jamaica's prominent and widely read newspaper to protest against the callous beatings.

Recaptured prisoners arrived at intervals for the rest of the day. The warders' brutal treatment continued until the supply of returned convicts was exhausted, as must have been the arms of the warders. Support Company maintained a guard there for many hours, quartered in a room above the courtyard. From here I watched the 'lifers' in the yard, wearing a red band on the sleeve on their white prison clothes, moving about freely without supervision. The warders had returned to their various tasks so the courtyard was virtually cleared, apart from the lifers' and the commotion when a man would be hurried through to a cell after being brought in from his brief liberty. The physical abuse did not cease.

The role played by the Royal Welch Fusiliers was scaled down but the battalion supplied a guard of ten men for nearly two weeks before the prison was considered under control. This was of no concern to me as after my duty on the morning after the hurricane I returned to Up Park camp and events led to Alex and I returning to Newcastle. As I saw things at that jail: the warders were vulnerable, with the many convicts on the loose and our presence was a wise precaution, but far more liberty was taken in the sadistic thrashings handed out which was witnessed by us, than surely was necessary. I am of the strong opinion our presence for these warders came down to an opportunity to settle many old scores and also contained an element of 'showing off' for our benefit.

Stories of the hurricane told of how at Port Royal a tidal wave washed into the bay, lifting several ships onto the roadway. At the Harman Barracks in Kingston, headquarters of the Jamaican battalion, men were extremely fortunate after their building collapsed, when the steel lockers in the room held up the collapsed roof. Even so, one man died at the Barracks and six were injured. The full death count for Hurricane Charlie – civilian and military – reached 152, with over 25,000 left homeless. After it left Jamaica it got as far as Yucatan in Mexico.

Later on, at Morant Bay where the Royal Welch were helping in relief work, a group of men came across a local fellow charging folk a penny to cross a coconut palm blown across an impassable river. The soldiers told the Jamaican that they thought this somewhat unjust, to which his answer was to cut the tree and to throw it in the swollen river. The military then proceeded into the man's garden, cutting down another palm which they placed over the water. The troops made sure the bridge was toll free.

Morant Bay was left without a shack standing. When Support Company saw it later, only a few badly damaged buildings were all that remained. All the banana palms were destroyed, along with many coconut ones. The local authorities worked very hard in co-operation with the Fusiliers and others to restore some kind of normality to the place. In contrast to many interested only in cashing in on the hurricane, relief poured in from Britain and elsewhere. HMS *Apollo*, then one of the fastest ships in the navy, made record time steaming out from Britain to bring relief supplies, such as blankets and tents, to Jamaica.

On the first day after the 'big wind', one of the tasks of the battalion was the distribution of drinking water to water points. The Fusiliers did this with the use of only one water truck and one trailer which is all it possessed. But the problem was too large to be solved this way and the battalion eventually had the use of big rum tankers from the Jamaica Sugar Association. The battalion was delivering up to 60,000 gallons of water a day when the Public Services took over the job after some ten days.

The post-hurricane period was very hectic. Of the 500 or so men of the Fusiliers in Kingston and Newcastle, some 300 each day found themselves involved in relief work in one way or another. The Red Cross set up relief centres, where the food had to be cooked, the water point guarded and first aid administered. Members of the Royal Welch band put down their instruments to assist with these and other tasks, ably assisted by men of Headquarter Company. Ladies of

Up Park camp (officers' wives and wives of other ranks) helped with the distribution of clothing and emergency food to the destitute, in reply to an appeal by the wife of the Governor, Lady Foot. The work involved a mixture of clerical, sorting of second hand clothing, some parcelling up of bundles and the delivery of goods. Much of this very welcome help was delivered through tracks impassable for civilian vehicles and at times there were difficult crowds to control. Fusilier Bingham acted in the dual role of bodyguard and driver whenever a party of wives took their mercy and relief into the hills. He and other drivers involved in these operations performed a lot of good work.

Just a little on hurricanes: the hurricane season for the Caribbean is during June to November of each year Way out in the Atlantic Ocean, storms build up in strength, move westwards and turn into hurricanes. Winds of these great storms can reach up to 300 kilometres per hour. These winds carry with them torrential rain, causing floods to be compared with the actual wind in damage caused. The centre of the hurricane is known as the 'eye', in which a strange calm prevails and the storm itself appears to diminish before the great storm continues. The very southern area of the Caribbean usually escapes the threat of these hurricanes. So, although the Caribbean in general enjoys a very temperate climate most of the year round, with lots of sunshine, it does not completely escape the ravages of nature.

A last footnote on the hurricane: the last thing to come over the radio on that night was a commercial for a well-known local firm of undertakers – not the best of omens. Mankind is inclined to believe it is in charge of most things but now and then nature proves a point; a point that was certainly proved at Jamaica on 17 August 1951. Jamaica has not known many greater hurricanes since that time.

6

Newcastle again

Soon after the hurricane Alex and I sat our exam and I had the most serious misgivings when confronted by the mathematics. We were told the results would not be immediately available and we could make our way to Newcastle to return to own company, on the condition we did so under our own resources as the road was still impassable in many spots. Alex and I, carrying kit bags on our shoulders, set off on the journey to the Blue Mountains, looking forward to being with our mates again even if it meant the semi-isolation of the hills.

My memory is hazy at this point but I believe we were given lifts by civilian vehicles before eventually reaching a point where we could by-pass the road and scramble up through the vegetation, finding ourselves near the camp. But this was not for some time. By the time we arrived the effort of the constant upward climb, with the task of carrying our gear, had us in a lather of sweat, with our jackets dark with the moisture, sticking to the skin. My feet ached to be free of the confinement of heavy boots, thick socks and the restriction of puttees. It was pretty warm in there. During our climb I found Alex as a companion as dour as ever, making another reason to be thankful on reaching our goal.

We were given a hearty welcome – exchanging tales about the hurricane before settling back to the familiar life we had previously known. The hurricane season had not passed and there was a lot of discussion about the possibility of other disasters, as the consequences of 'Charlie' were mopped up at Newcastle and elsewhere on the island. With many people homeless and living under canvas, it would be a very bad time for another big storm to strike. The population listened to weather forecasts anxiously.

Bob McIntyre, an 'old soldier', was very partial to the booze, often finding himself in difficult situations because of it. And so it was – he got stabbed in the arm one night, drinking rum in a civilian watering hole some three kilometres or so from our camp. How he got to this bar, sharing his company with his Jamaican companions is another story but things certainly went wrong that night and the old regular turned up at camp with a very bloody wound.

There was a great deal of talk on the matter before the blood rushed to our heads and the we decided in anger to travel over to the scene of the crime to avenge our fellow soldier. Armed with sturdy sticks, a gang of about thirty of us made our way along the main road leading out of the camp. I have often pondered why Corporal James accompanied us, as it would incriminate him too. On reflection, his defence would have been that he came with us to control the situation. We travelled a mile or two before striking out up a mountain track, up then down, over several valleys, before we were able to look down on a collection of wooden buildings which included the bar which Bob McIntyre had frequented. Although Bob was not with us, of course, his close friends were and knew where to guide us. The talk of revenge had bubbled as in a cauldron as we had trekked over the hills, so we were ripe for action as we descended the slope towards the small hamlet. A few locals stood around, uncertain of what our intentions were, but they appeared docile and offered no serious threat of opposing us, we thought.

One man, saying he was the owner of the bar, pushed himself forward to offer his explanation of the night before but we were not interested in listening to him. Our brains had shut down to any entreaty to reason, with only the thought of revenge clouding our thinking. The small crowd stood impassive as we entered the bar, making it obvious we were looking for trouble. It took just one of us to lash out with a stick at some of the fittings inside, before everyone joined in an orgy of destruction. Even Corporal James, I noticed, was carried away with the fever of mob rule, lashing out with the best of us. Standing on the bar counter to reach the bottles on shelves, soldiers of the Royal Welch Fusiliers did not serve him well that day, as the bar echoed to the noises of men smashing all in their vision, to an accompaniment of coarse language peppered with the blows. I can remember the obscene sense of power as I wielded my club about me. It was possible to see the silent people outside watching the mayhem and I suddenly felt foolish and somewhat sorry for the people watching, particularly the bar owner. This awareness caused the exhilaration to leave me as quickly as air from a pricked balloon. I continued to smash things, but the heart had gone out of it for me. The hapless bar owner stood watching the destruction, a look of stunned disbelief at our actions. He said nothing, as we moved out into the open, to begin the climb up the slope. He stood watching us as we made our way back to barracks. On the journey many of us told of what we had experienced in the smashing of the bar but I also felt a nervousness beneath the comments, as we feared, inwardly, the results of the vandalism. Ever since this incident I have understood the effects of a mob mentality, how easily common sense can desert you in the face of irrational appeals, how you can be led by mob rule, swept along, breathing only anger. We had only showed concern for the stabbing of one of our own, not questioning further the actions of Bob McIntyre – no choirboy. It can be said no one deserves to be knifed regardless, but mob revenge is not the answer and we were to learn we had destroyed a man's bar simply because the offence had taken place on his premises. But the bar owner did not sit back and accept his fate. He contacted Newcastle camp, and who could blame him.

Drifting back into camp, in groups, our sticks thrown away, we arrived to find news of our adventure had preceded us. Our commanding officer, Major Bosanquet, was furious with us and he had us line up before him on the square. He warned us that soldiers acting like children deserved to be treated as such. We were told our job was to prevent violence and not to promote it. The admonishment ended with an order of extra guards over the following days for all of us. Looking back at it today, I feel we were let off lightly.

The guards went on for a few days before hurricane warnings of another possible threat to Jamaica diverted attention away from our crime, as preparations were made for another emergency. The storm did not come our way and our life returned to normal, the extra duties forgotten or forgiven. No doubt the Army paid compensation to the unlucky bar owner and no more was heard of the issue. The event is not one I remember with pride, showing how individuals can throw reason out of the window, to commit acts of sheer stupidity. It shows how individual dogs in a pack, become a pack of wild dogs, doing things alien to them in a normal situation. I never heard anything about Corporal James's part in our raid and he still continued to be our corporal.

Soon afterwards I got the news that I had failed the Education course exam I had taken in Kingston which may have surprised many other people but not me. Our friend Alex had got through. Many chaps in my barrack room did not or could not believe I had failed the exam as I think that they thought of me as something of a barrack-room lawyer but I tried to explain that I had no head for mathematics. Now I was made an assistant storeman at our company store, to help in the issue of equipment to cadre participants, among other tasks. He was Fusilier Williams, treble one, (the last three digits of his army number). I was required to move in and sleep on the store premises, living a life of reasonable comfort, away from the barrack-room. (Soldiers in the battalion were generally addressed by their name and the last three digits of their army number, especially in 'Part 2', or routine, orders. I was known as Stevens 606.)

I found Williams (another Englishman) to be on the weird side. He laughed too much at his own jokes, which were mostly not that funny. He would roar with laughter, in a voice that grated, at some of his utterances, forcing the listener to join in his strange sense of humour: sometimes difficult to do, but done perhaps in politeness. This side of him apart, I found him reasonable to share quarters with and life progressed in a good state of affairs for a little while.

Now may be the time to pause and look some more into the background of Jamaica and its people at the time. Around seventy five percent of them were of Negro blood. Maybe about seventeen per cent were of mixed descent, with one percent white. The remainder would be a mixture of East Indian, Chinese and others.

The island's Negroes had originally been brought from Africa as slaves by the Spanish. But slavery was continued and developed by the British after their capture of the island. They had been badly treated, beginning by being chained hand and foot, before the branding of the slave trader's mark on their skin. The slaves were taken below to the holds of the ships, which meant poor sanitation and ventilation. Many of the wretches would not survive the voyage, with those who did condemned to a lifetime of humiliation and degradation, sometimes separated from families when sold and taken off to sugar plantations. The slaves would be grouped into gangs before going out to the fields where they would prepare the earth, before planting the sugar cane. Later they would cut the cane and bundle it. Slaves would be employed at the sugar factories, grinding the cane, boiling the sugar, before filling the barrels with sugar for export overseas. If a slave was lucky he or she could be taken on as a servant by one of the wealthy landowners. Being even luckier, they could be treated well, becoming in time a valued family asset: but always a possession. Lots of white owners used female slaves for their gratification: hence the beginning of a large mixed race population.

When Spain had taken possession of its discoveries in the Caribbean it was anxious to keep the wealth to itself. Columbus had been searching for a new route to Asia and he called the islands the West Indies, thinking he had hit on the west way to India. Discovering his error, Columbus, now aware the world was a bigger place than had been envisaged, still realised the opportunities for himself and for Spain. An empire could be built, developing Spain into a powerful force in Europe. Spain set out to protect its conquests by the King appealing to the Pope to justify their claim to the West Indies. A rightful claim as the Spanish viewed things. The Pope obligingly put his name to the Treaty of Tordesilas which drew an imaginary line through the Atlantic Ocean from north to south. The lands to the West of this line (discovered by Spain) were to be designated as Spanish territory. The same treaty allowed the Portuguese to claim possession of lands to the East of the line.

Spain had a colossal task to keep its territories, as other European countries wanted to share the spoils, usually the way of things and trouble in Europe became an excuse to attack Spanish possessions in the Caribbean. Spanish warships (galleons) sailed the seas in an attempt to keep out the unwelcome visitors. Europeans had become accustomed to the taste of tobacco so the Spanish treasure ships became an attraction for this commodity, apart from the usual meaning of treasure. The English became a player in these games, with famous names such as Francis Drake, Henry Morgan and Edward Teach becoming rich in their plundering of the Spanish Main. The British used men like Morgan as privateers who attacked Spanish vessels to capture the gold being conveyed from South America. The actions of these men did much to weaken Spanish power in the Caribbean, but even so, at the closing of the sixteenth century Spain remained the dominant European nation in that part of the world. The Spanish Main was still held.

The Dutch broke the grip of the Spanish. At the commencement of the seventeenth century they began trading with Venezuela for salt and later tobacco. This extended to trade with Guyana and eventually the West Indian islands. The Dutch set up a Dutch West India Company, with their ships sailing the area to protect their trading stations. In the year 1629 the Spanish suffered a great loss to the Dutch, when they lost an entire treasure fleet, which marked the beginning of the end for Spanish domination. The Spanish had never known such a disaster. Now the British and French settled colonies in the eastern Caribbean, while still attacking the Spanish settlements and, as time passed, the Spanish supremacy began to ebb. Although it had been the Dutch who had broken the stranglehold, it was the British who became the biggest colonisers in the area. Jamaica was the biggest island in what was to become known as the British West Indies. As for Spain, for most of the twentieth century, it was one of the poorest nations in Europe. Where did all that gold go?

As these events unfolded, more and more slaves poured into the West Indies, eventually becoming the most numerous part of the population on the island of Jamaica. They brought with them from Africa diseases such as Yellow Fever, which hit their white masters hard, not being familiar with such ills, which took a toll on their number. There were several slave revolts on the island and much cruel treatment for rebels when captured. This treatment could include limbs being hacked from the body, one by one until eventual death. A terrible example for those inclined to take the same revolutionary path.

The stores at Newcastle provided a life for me excused such duties as night guards and life was good for a while, if maybe a little dull. One Saturday afternoon, a long weekend ahead with nowhere really to go, Williams 111 (treble one) and I got into the Captain Morgan rum. We sat in the locked storeroom in our sleeping quarters, getting gradually pickled. Being Saturday afternoon, there was little, if any, chance of being disturbed, so we babbled on, probably talking a lot of rubbish as the rum took effect. Sometime well into the afternoon I left the stores, clutching a rum bottle, well used, making my way towards the square. Williams 111 was left behind, probably sleeping it off. Looking back, I have no idea of my intentions, but I was once again in the hold of rum and capable of anything. I came across a Jamaican market woman walking with her basket across the edge of the square, towards the road leading out of the camp. In my drunken stupor, after weeks of isolation in the hills, I saw her as sexually appealing, but suspect now she may have been well past her prime. I was aflame with the rum however, and pushed my attentions on her, wildly waving the almost empty rum bottle in the air, as I slurred my words in the form of a direct request for sex. She was not interested and kept trying to get away from me and leave the camp. But with the arrogance of youth and the alcohol, I persisted, as I walked along the road, leaving the camp behind us, sensing she was beginning to find some merit in the idea. I kept up the pressure, probably offering her a small sum, before she finally conceded and put down her basket from her head, the usual way Jamaican women transported anything. We left the road a little way, the basket full of bananas pushed under some bushes, climbing down into the undergrowth on the side of the mountain falling away from the road. Here I groped her in a most unromantic way, interested only in satisfying my drunken urges. The whole act, probably my first experience of sex, was a most mechanical one, purely one of release. At the end of the process, the woman lost her appeal for me, now anxious to be away and back to the camp. She was keen to continue her journey, so the whole thing had been one of mutual need only; hers for a pittance. I for my part, for a few minutes of pleasure, would spend many days ahead worrying and looking out for the first signs of VD. Not much of a bargain. I have often wondered since if she may have become pregnant. I am not proud of this disclosure.

Christmas arrived, which for us was not much more than an excuse for a good old booze up, and some time to ourselves, being given Christmas and Boxing days off. I spent some time in the barrack rooms, having a drink here and there, and during one of these sessions, a very young black girl appeared at the entrance to the room. She would have been, perhaps, seventeen, and to be frank about it, did not look the full quid. Some conversation with her established that she was weak-minded at the least, and was prepared to have sex with anyone for whatever bones we would throw her, so to speak. Before long she was stretched out on a spare mattress on an unused wire bed, being given the treatment by a Fusilier. Most of us were full of the Christmas spirit, as we spurred him on to glory. As one soldier lay on top of her giving his all, we cheered wildly, with one lad covering the two leading players in talcum powder, before someone threw an army blanket over them. The blanket moved up and down for some time, with the white powder coming away in small puffs through the wool. The girl seemed happy in her job, and was sent away in due course with some small offerings. Once again it was a case of supply and demand.

Some time later, soldiering again at Newcastle, I saw this same girl hanging around the camp. It was during an NCOs' cadre, of which I was a member, and I remember one evening when she dispensed her services inside one of the toilets within the camp. A long stream of men waited patiently in line to enjoy her favours. I cannot decide now which was the most degrading, the girl herself selling her body for peanuts, or the men taking her one by one, without even the benefit of a shower in between, or the protection of a rubber, with few men of those days carrying or caring to use them in spite of army pressure to wear them. Inside the darkness of the toilet, this young girl repeatedly gave herself to a flood of semen in such a casual manner, it is difficult, these years later, to believe it happened, and that these men could have put themselves so far into the gutter, with all concerned highly at risk from VD. I do not wish to be too judgmental – I am a man too – but if it shows anything, it is the depths to which fit, young men will go to satisfy their needs and how a young black girl, living in abject poverty would only be too anxious to join them. I doubt if she was paid very much. Looking back, I find hard to believe such things happened but I assure you that they did.

'C' Company had lived at Newcastle for a longer period than expected. It had been my home, apart from the hurricane period, since my arrival in Jamaica. I had an affinity with the peace of the place: the stillness of the days and the temperate weather. We had a relaxing of discipline, and a good community spirit. True, there were periods of boredom, but it was possible to apply for a weekend pass to Kingston if so desired but somehow I never bothered. There were the visits to the 'one-reel' film shows, books to read and perhaps too much alcohol to swallow. One night a group of us were given an invitation to a local dance, out of the camp, somewhere down the mountain. The participants were Jamaicans from the small settlements around Newcastle, some probably from the small hamlet where we had demolished most of the bar. The dance floor was nothing more than a stone courtyard, not terribly large. It was out in the open, with a ramshackle, wooden home at one edge of the courtyard. All around, in the very dark night, there were kerosene lamps to light the way to the calypsos being danced, the stirring music played by the small local calypso band. The faces of the dancers, some as black as Welsh coal, others coffee-coloured, showed the sweat pouring from their brows, as they moved to the music, maybe taking them subconsciously back to their roots in Africa. But the descendants of African slaves had formed their own culture over time and the calypso was one of the products. In the friendly, warm glow of the lamps, a happy Jamaican gave a rendering of a popular calypso of the time:

Brown Skinned Girl stay home and mind baby,
Brown Skinned Girl stay home and mind baby,
Your Daddy's gone on a sailing boat,
And if he don't come back,
Stay home and mind baby...

The calypso would evolve into reggae over the next couple of decades, with its prime exponent, Bob Marley.

More people came as the night progressed, and by about 10p.m. the place was jumping. A seething mass of sweating individuals – including we few Welshmen – dancing, frenzy-like, to the irresistible music. Living, mostly, a hard life, the Jamaicans knew how to play; with the women writhing in a very sensual way, full of promise of things that might happen. The drink was flowing freely, escaping quickly in the sweat of the dances. There was no trouble: everyone intent only on enjoying the evening. It was a happy time, that night, and has stayed long in memory. I admired very much the easy grace of the Jamaican dancers, the rhythm and the blatant sexual approach. It all came so natural for them; examples of which I would see over and over, of how these people could slip into the calypso mode, torsos swiveling to that happy sound, dark faces creased in big-toothed smiles.

I remember another dance at Newcastle, this time at the camp itself. It was held at the Church Hall, the cinema venue. It was only for military personnel, including married families residing on the mountain. One of our officers had married a lady from another West Indian country. It may have been the island of Grenada, but I am not certain, but a detachment of Fusiliers had been sent there, a potential trouble spot, at an early stage of the battalion's stint in the Caribbean.

I was told of how some members of this detachment had come across the famous John Wayne, Hollywood film hero, bathing in the surf. He had been friendly and hospitable, making a good impression on the men talking to him. At that time, of course, John Wayne would have been at the very apex of his career and world famous for his tough guy and cowboy roles.

To return to the dance at Newcastle: I remember how fascinated I was with the officer's new wife. She was white, dainty, gentle and most beautiful. She kicked off her shoes, dancing with all ranks, moving around the slippery wooden floor in her stockings. To me she was a mirage of loveliness and it was evident why she had captivated her husband. The sheer stockings showed off perfect legs. For me, it was instant love, or lust, that stayed with me the whole evening. It was an emotional package that was never going to go anywhere and I was probably in company with most of the men present. I remember this woman as a vision of unobtainable sexiness, probably as a teenager may secretly desire his teacher's attractions, with the bitter-sweet arrow to the breast; the little boy at the window of the sweet shop with an empty pocket but full of longing. I never saw the woman after that night but I remember it was one of the many times I fell in love as a young man, not knowing what love really was but reaching out with feelings, mixed with a great deal of lust, in the flexing of youthful passions.

And so for the present, my days at Newcastle came to a close. I would serve there again but not as a member of 'C' Company. On Company Orders one afternoon I received the order to attend a driving course at Kingston. I assumed I would then become a member of the battalion's Motor Transport Section if I got through my test. So again I got set to packing my kit, once more to ride the ration truck to the city. The next time I returned to do duty in Newcastle all my mates in 'C' Company were gone, and by that time probably de-mobbed as they were national servicemen.

7

Kingston on wheels

Candidates for the driving course came from different companies of the Royal Welch. There were probably some ten of us, gathered together, and placed in the same billet, in that part of the camp occupied by the MT Section. This was in an ideal spot, near the swimming pool, and the guardhouse, where we were required to sign in and out when leaving through the big iron gates, flanked on either side by two old cannons.

In front of the guardhouse stood the flagpole, from which fluttered the Union Jack, taken down each evening to the playing of 'retreat' by the duty bugler. We did in fact serve under a flag lacking any Welsh symbol or design – the Union Jack, described by some as the butcher's apron. It represented the English, Scots and the Irish but that was the end of it. But in those days, most of us were not terribly conscious of such things, having gone through a school system imparting to us the glories of the British empire, with the school maps showing so much of the world in pink: Britannia ruled the waves, and these pink countries showed its power and influence. Nowadays the Welsh are, I believe, far more involved in their own individuality as a people and as a nation, the days of empire glory now passed; perhaps it is time to have another look at ourselves.

As a young man without any particular politics I was happy enough to serve under the Union Jack and there were many Englishmen and others in my battalion. It was basically a Welsh battalion, with much singing of Welsh songs. Although it was good to sing 'There'll always be an England' and 'Maybe it's because I'm a Londoner', it was important to me and to many others that we were Welsh. I loved to sing in my mangled Welsh in our many sing-songs. While most of the battalion's other ranks were Welsh, I found that the officers to be otherwise: mostly English. But they always did their duty on St David's Day, serving us our special dinner as was our regimental custom.

I was to find a couple of our party had done a lot of driving in civilian life. I had some driving experience myself, having previously done a course when first entering the army. This had been during my service with the 14th/20th Hussars at Catterick. At the end of the course I was told that I had come sixth or seventh in the course, and was eligible to go to Germany as a driver. As I related, the army frowned on my friendship with Trooper Russell, who went to Hong Kong. Although lucky in our proximity to the pool, there was also a disadvantage. The billet next to ours being the sleeping quarters of the battalion band, which gave us an unwelcome intimacy to their practising and tuning their instruments.

The initial part of the course was at Up Park camp, on roads not frequently used. Here we began to learn to drive from an elementary stage, we experienced ones on the same level as those who had not been behind the wheel ever. There was also some written work, on the workings of the combustion engine, so there was enough to keep us occupied and we were lucky to escape guard duties for the term of the course.

We were free to leave the camp in the evenings or weekends, most of us preferring to wear civilian clothes on our excursions into the city. After six months service you were eligible to wear 'civvies' after duties, which in the climate of Jamaica was a relaxed rule of shirt and pants, and sandals or shoes. Many of us wore the brightly coloured shirts available locally, covered in the names of Jamaican tourist spots in vivid print. We effectively joined the calypso society, wearing its badge of happy apparel. It was possible to apply for a permanent pass which allowed leave from the camp (unless detailed for duties) from noon on a Saturday to 6 a.m. on the Monday following. If placed on a charge (put on a 252, known by its Army form number) and found guilty, rights to civilian clothes and a permanent pass would be withdrawn.

Leaving camp on a Saturday night, with the best intentions of staying circumspect, a group of us could, after a series of rums, find ourselves at a bar such as 'The Blue Orchid' in Hanover Street, a notorious street of brothels in downtown Kingston. The evening would become a time of sitting around a table, in the usually bare surroundings of a bar with perhaps a fan cutting through the humid air. Those who wanted beer – cold, out of the ice chest – drank Red Stripe, others preferred rum, generally with Coke. There would be two or three women sitting at another table, in various shades of colour and size, making it obvious they were available for sexual entertainment – for a price. On a shelf near the bar, probably behind it, a Bakelite radio broadcasting Radio Jamaica might be throwing out the words, from a woman singer, singing the calypso:

> Please Mister – don't you touch my tomato,
> touch me on my pumpkin or potato
> but don't you touch my tomato.
> (The pronunciation of tomato was in the American way: toe-mate-oh)

As the evening moved on in a flow of alcohol, the women in the bar would begin to look more attractive and appealing, provided they were still around, not having found other partners, as we would not necessarily be the only troops drinking there. If you found yourself attracted to one of the women, the usual gambit would be to offer to buy a drink for the lady, to discover any electricity passing between the two of you or not. If the spark were there, negotiations on sex would start almost at once. If you knew you had made an error, and the woman lost her appeal, you would excuse yourself, visit the toilet and move in on a different target. If this was not possible, it would be a matter of returning to your table, making enough signals to your former choice to move on to other pastures. It was all very crude and casual. If your lady was what you wanted, the negotiations, after agreeing on sex, would run to 'short time' or 'all night.' So far as the soldier was concerned, it mostly came down to what funds were available, with an all night session probably meaning no more money until the next pay parade. Flushed with drink, a hasty decision could carry much regret in the bright light of the following morning, financially and otherwise. There was always the fear of catching VD.

Having decided maybe on a short time, it was customary to pay up front, before the woman of your desires would lead the way to a room elsewhere in the building. A room, small and sparse, with a bed but no bedding other than sheets and a pillow. Beneath the bed would usually be a china chamber pot in which to empty the bladder, most urgent because of the drink, before rising to the occasion. Some ladies of the night, I suppose you could call them, were more fastidious than others, carrying in an enamel bowl, with soap and towel, to wash your private parts before and after the deed. This had certain virtue but was no real protection from syphilis and other infections.

The act itself did not last long. These women of the bars knew how to move themselves and bring a man quickly to orgasm. Besides, the urgency of the male made a large contribution, provided not too much alcohol had been absorbed beforehand. There were no restrictions on the paying customer, such as having to wear a condom (these were days long before AIDS came on the scene, though it was still risky). There would be perhaps many clients for the backyard abortionists or perhaps a half-caste baby in the offing. Most of these women were 'street wise', of course, knowing the tricks of the trade and pregnancy was just another hazard in the game they played.

Very few, if any, of the local men frequented the bars. Apart from soldiers, the clientele consisted of a small number of merchant seamen (I once spent a good time in the company of some young Germans who seemed desperate for our friendship), and also sailors of the American navy, on furlough from their base in Cuba (Guantanamo Bay). There was a friendly rivalry between us and the Americans. Most of the time, the Fusiliers had these places to themselves, with the local men having their own places of vice among the darkened streets of bustling Kingston. They kept to their side of the fence and we to ours.

The time arrived, during our course, to venture out of Up Park camp. We graduated to the peaceful roads on the outskirts of the city (in those days of the early 'fifties not too many locals could afford a motor car). Most of the day was spent in the back of a truck as we all had our turn at the wheel. We would be given sandwiches from the cookhouse to see us through to the evening meal, stopping at a pleasant spot to enjoy the culinary delights of a greasy bacon sandwich or the like, followed by a satisfying smoke. Many of us were not too proud, if being broke, to ask someone for 'two's up,' an expression asking for a few drags at a cigarette before the owner threw it away. Sometimes you might request a 'two's up,' only to be told it had already been booked by another member of the party and it might mean missing out on a smoke altogether. If you were flush with funds at that particular time, it would not be a good idea to carry too many cigarettes or cash on you, as you became an instant target for those waiting for pay day. If you were too generous, you finished up being mean to yourself. Many times, I remember being out of smokes and money, when taking delivery of a letter from my father containing, as usual, one of those thin packets of Woodbines consisting of five (flattened) cigarettes between the written pages. A lifebelt to a sinking man, indeed. My father had served during the Second World War through the African and Italian campaigns and he probably remembered the hours without a cigarette. I will always thank him for this consideration, and the joy of being handed such a letter by the post corporal on those bleak days. If we were away from the billet, as we were when learning to drive, the mail would be placed on your bed for your return, a sight to lift your heart, indeed.

Our vehicle did not have modern day technology of course, with the clutch having to be used in a double movement when changing gears. Gears had to be changed with a certain precision, or it would not happen without the most terrible grindings: what we called playing the national anthem. A chap called Morgan was about the best driver of the lot of us, with much pre-army experience: a very funny Fusilier, absolutely refusing to take the army or life seriously. Great fun this man.

Tom and Morgan (46) 'the best driver of the lot of us ... great fun this man'.

We had to make our direction signals by hand, and the sergeant in charge did not take kindly to a signal to turn left turning out to be a right turn instead. Apart from the sergeant, there was a corporal to assist him: both members of REME (the Royal Electrical and Mechanical Engineers) attached to the battalion. These REME men maintained the Fusiliers' vehicles at the MT yard at Up Park camp in the large workshop bays there. They were easy to get along with for most of the time, apart from those occasions one of us would threaten to wreck our truck, either by a fine rendering of 'God Save the King' on the gears, or heading straight for the nearest palm trees. All bets were off then, with the juiciest of language telling you where to go. You went to the back of the truck to lick your wounds in silence and deep embarrassment with your mates probably secretly glad, as it kept them in the running for a licence and the prospect of a 'cushy' time of things in the MT Section. But on balance we all picked things up fairly well, as time passed, moving towards the deciding test by the officer in charge of Motor Transport, Captain Davies. His reputation as a grump with a 'fly-off-the-handle' temper preceded him, as he joined our group to give us a try out before the test proper. He offered no encouragement, sitting stiffly in his seat with a sullen attitude, as though willing the driver to make a mess of things. People would get so flustered by his surly disposition, they were likely to make mistakes, (such as stalling the truck) they would not normally make. Captain Davies was responsible for the MT, but most troops were aware it was the MT Sergeant: Sergeant Foulkes and his cronies (especially one corporal, whom we suspected of being homosexual) who ran the section. Captain Davies was not a popular officer and with his approach to things, did not deserve to be.

He was a short, ginger-mustached individual with a clipped, abrupt manner of speech. There were no shades other than black and white for this man; and I have a very intense memory of his poor attitude to men and ability to bring the worst out of people. If ever an officer would have been shot in battle by his own men it would have been Captain Davies. He has probably joined that great army in the sky by this time (he was about forty something then) and I wonder on his popularity there. I wouldn't be surprised if Adolf Hitler had asked for his services in the Royal Hell Fusiliers! But enough about him, let us move on to the test, even if he had to be the examining officer.

I did not do well but did not exactly fail. I was kept on for extra tuition, before taking a supplementary test with Corporal Williams. The afternoon came when I climbed into a jeep, ready to set off for the hectic, busy shopping centre of Kingston during the peak time of the day, with the corporal in the seat next to me. He was from the Rhondda Valley, as Welsh as they come, possessing a big mop of red hair and a face covered in freckles. I found him relaxed, which made me relaxed, and a most friendly companion. I was pleased by his comment on my driving, stating how good was my clutch control as we negotiated the bustling streets, full of locals walking in the centre of the road, in the many, many places where there was no pavement of any kind. The corporal told me I had passed the test with flying colours. From that moment, I became a Driver Class 3, an official member of the staff of the MT Section. I had left 'C' Company behind, up there on the hills, and so became a Fusilier of Headquarter Company, the parent company of the battalion drivers. However, I was to find that the older members of MT Section were very jealous of their seniority and it proved very difficult for a new member of the MT to do much driving.

The battalion mounted a guard of honour for HRH Princess Alice, the Princess Royal. Another guard was provided by 'A' Company for Rear Admiral Greer of the United States Navy. There was lots of what we knew as 'bull' (probably a shortened version of bullshit), with boots shining like glass and cap badges and other brasses catching the Jamaican sun, throwing out arrows of glinting light. Freshly washed hackles and newly pressed flashes added to the picture of military near-perfection. It was the blue beret itself that seemed to 'seal-in' a man's smartness, I always thought. Some of us had a way of wearing them, and presenting them, never followed by a certain group of individuals, with berets, too large (not properly shrunk) and sticking out to the right like a wing, all puffy and silly-looking. The ideal beret seemed to be worn on the ideal shaped head, shrunk to the shape leaving little surplus material to hang over the side. The usual way to shrink the berets was a process of putting the headwear through a mixture of hot and cold water when new. Some had the knack of it, many did not: and I think I came somewhere in the middle, not looking ridiculous as some but not the smartest soldier ever to pull on a beret. The main thing was of course, to pass inspection on parade and avoid having an officer standing before you crying out: 'Take this man's name, Sergeant!' – bad music to the ears indeed.

Early one morning we awoke to hear of the death of the King. The radio went into mourning, playing only classical music for the next twenty-four hours. I wondered if they would do that in Britain itself. The late king, George VI, had died on 6 February 1952, shortly after the Princess Elizabeth and her husband, the Duke of Edinburgh, had flown to Africa. They were returning to Britain to honour the King, with the Princess also being the next in royal line. The battalion's Anti-tank Platoon fired a salute to the King on the day the news came through and at a later time when the Proclamation Parade was held. A memorial service for the King was held at the Cathedral in Spanish Town on a fine old-fashioned square. The guard of honour was commanded by Major the Lord Wynford (our officer at the prison). In attendance also, were officers of the garrison, the Royal Navy, and also the Jamaica Regiment. The Governor, Sir Hugh Foot, in all his colonial regalia, was received by the Guard, before it went marching off, in slow time, to the Cathedral; inside of which sat the notables of Jamaica with their ladies. The Lord Bishop of Jamaica took the service, a very impressive one. The Jamaica Regiment's band played in its Zouave-style full dress, which also made a deep impression on those present, which included 300 men from the Fusiliers. As the monarch had also been the Colonel-in-Chief of the Fusiliers, as well as our king, this was a big affair in the day-to-day happenings of the battalion, and it was indeed 'bull' of the highest level. The badge of the Royal Welch Fusiliers, known to us with affection as 'the flaming piss-pot', had probably never gleamed so brightly as in this farewell to the King. 'The King is dead – long live the Queen!' was the toast in the Officers' Mess, I presume.

For us new members of the MT, there was little duty in the way of driving. With the regular work was taken by the old hands, we new recruits found ourselves spending most of our time cleaning vehicles with a mixture of kerosene and oil. When buffed up with a clean rag, this formula gave very good results, in a shine so beloved by the Army, and which showed a vehicle at its best. We were not over-stretched in our labours and life continued on a not-too-difficult path. There were afternoons at the swimming pool, not much being done throughout the battalion in the heat of the day, where we could splash about and doze near the kiosk where ice cold drinks and chocolate, frozen among the chunks of ice in a large chest, were available if you were financially viable. Steel tables and chairs were set out on the white, concrete sun deck above the pool, from which access to the two different heights of the diving tower was possible. The kiosk was usually in the care of a Jamaican worker employed by the camp NAAFI, as it was an extension of the NAAFI, in the matter of supply and profit. At the base of the pool nearby, sat the souvenir sellers, also where the wash/starch and iron women carried out their business, all with the approval of the law-dispensers of the battalion. The souvenirs included the gaudy cushion covers with 'JBWI' (Jamaica, British West Indies) embroidered in, different brightly coloured cottons, probably more at home in a Bedouin's tent in the desert than the United Kingdom of 1952 where most of the covers would end up: presents to families, wife or girlfriend far across the sea.

Life at the MT settled into a routine of odd jobs, a visit to the cinema, and the odd night out in the bars and brothels, both really the same thing. The golden age of Hollywood, with its 'Studio System' of stars tied to its bosom, was coming to a close but few were yet aware of the growing baby called television, gaining strength as the 'fifties moved on. I remember at this time sending to Hollywood for a picture of Esther Williams, the famous swimming star, and in due course I did receive a photograph from her studio with Esther Williams posing in a swim-suit on a diving board. I kept the picture for many years but somehow it got lost as the years rolled by.

Stars of the calibre of Humphrey Bogart and Lauren Bacall were featured in plays broadcast by Radio Jamaica in between the advertising jingles allowed on this station. Nat 'King' Cole sat at the top of popularity at that time with others like Johnny Ray, Slim Whitman, Bing Crosby, Rosemary Clooney, Doris Day and Connie Francis offering stiff competition. The movie sensation known as Mario Lanza was taking the world by storm; with the partnership of Howard Keel and Kathryn Grayson turning out such musicals as Jerome Kern's *Showboat*.

One of the stars of this film, Ava Gardner, was conducting an on and off affair around the world with the fiery Frank Sinatra. We were still singing his kind of music, much like that of our parents, but standing in the wings was a phenomenon called Elvis Presley who, with his rock and roll, would change popular music forever.

I was getting to know better my companions from the driving course, those of us who had got through, sharing a billet and working together day by day. There was Morgan (46), a bundle of fun whose favourite party trick was to walk through the shower room, or even around the barrack room, with a towel draped over his erect penis, making enquiries on the location of his towel, saying he was unable to find it. He had the most wicked grin, with eyes of sparkling blue, full of mischief. You were never sure if he was telling you the truth or spinning one of his many fanciful stories. I have often thought that he could have got himself a serious injury if some Fusilier had made a grab for his towel.

Tom's mates, Thomas (89) ('another man with a good sense of humour'), and Morgan (46), 'a very funny fusilier'.

Thomas (89) was another man with a good sense of humour. He only possessed one testicle, so he said, and would cheerfully tell you that its loss was the legacy of climbing a spiked, steel fence as a youngster and getting himself impaled. It did not have much effect on his love life, being a good-looking character with an Errol Flynn (the famous swashbuckling film actor of the period) moustache and an insatiable desire to copulate. Thomas had a good muscular body, of which he was proud, and he often moved around flexing his muscles which seemed to create a quicksilver movement in his body, as the muscles bounced all around him. Like myself, he was fond of using a pencil and his work was good, individual, and strong lined. The man took little to heart with most of his disasters, and there were some, breaking through to a sunny day, when things, for him, had looked very dark indeed. He could charm the pants off a lady, which he had probably done many times before and would do again, taking the most appalling risks, in Jamaica, even if he had to pay for it there, with the women more interested in hard cash. I am certain he came down with a 'packet' – our term for VD – more than once, but after a shot or two with penicillin in the backside, the randy dandy would once again join the fray: making a connection with any woman prepared to open her legs for a price. I met him in a street in Swansea years later, seemingly unchanged, going through the game of life with a wink. If he has, by this time, moved on to the big pasture in the sky, I feel certain he will be doing his utmost to cast an angel or two, plus himself, into the eternal hell of damnation. Thomas – I thank you for those times of fun, making those Jamaican days and nights very memorable for me and others.

Another one of the crew was Fusilier Barber, a massive man, built like a Centurion tank, with shoulders as wide as the proverbial barn door. He was straight talking, honest and a little slow in his reactions which was really a virtue, as he thought things through carefully before responding. A good solid soldier, he would be the man for any emergency.

Fusilier Clifford – another of our merry men – was a fellow handed a rough deal in the looks department. He had a very wide mouth, with large teeth to match, giving the impression of having a grand piano behind big, fleshy lips. His loud and hyena-like laugh showed these features to their best disadvantage: and the man himself stood on two outsize feet, notorious for their pungent odour. Unfortunately he looked a bit of a fool and a great deal of the time he confirmed this opinion but he had a serious side – always prepared to do you a favour, with the ability too, of rounding quickly on those who took him for too much of a fool.

A chap called Cowell, a Londoner by birth but having spent a lot of time in Wales, was seen as a bit of a sneak, always ready to protect his own posterior. With large, round glasses, he was reminiscent of the silent film comedian, Harold Lloyd; also giving him a school teacher appearance to complement his know-everything approach to most things, with an attitude of having done everything at some time or another during his extremely short life. He was not the most popular member of our group, but was bearable in small doses, some of the time.

The last member of our gang was a tall, gangly bloke we knew as Thomas, (79). He always seemed to want to do the right thing, being all things to all men, wearing a false smile, I thought, and was not a man completely trustworthy. I feel – looking back – his problem was one of self esteem and insecurity and he was basically a decent soldier, often feeling out of his depth in things, putting on a front of confidence that did not fool the majority of us. His big failing was to let someone take the blame or not to stand behind an issue, if he saw any threat to his position.

These, then, were some of the men with whom I shared a barrack room, often walking to the showers or the cookhouse, carrying our two plates each, with cutlery in our pockets. We would go to the camp cinema together or maybe spend an hour at the NAAFI, the swimming pool, or even a longer time on a Saturday night doing a tour of the bars in the murky light of downtown Kingston. There were certainly others we had much contact with but these men were members of our driving course, progressing together into the MT.

One fellow – not in our group – was an overweight Englishman, probably a Londoner, called Endean, who could talk and spin a yarn like a second-hand car salesman. He had served in Jamaica before our battalion's arrival, marrying a local girl. He had been allowed to stay on in Jamaica, becoming attached to the Royal Welch, in the MT. The man always seemed to be in trouble in one form or another, using his persuasive gift of the gab to get himself out of it.

Corporal Merriman was so polite and civil – too smooth by half. The word was he was an 'arse bandit', in army lingo, and his 'boyfriend' also belonged to the MT; a much younger man than Merriman who would have been about thirty: his young lover, twenty something. Everyone amused themselves at these two when they conversed so sweetly on duty. Corporal Merriman was always good to many of us, if not all, but he had a sickly, almost feminine approach, which, together with the belief of his alleged homosexuality, gave most people the creeps, myself included. If his homosexuality was never proved, he was a strange, weird sort of a chap, with a complex personality hard to see the bottom of, so to speak. The corporal was always well dressed, smelling as sweet as his attitude.

Now came the time for me to move on for a while, to leave Jamaica, to join the MT personnel in Belize, British Honduras, attached to 'D' Company. I was given instructions to join the small service craft, operated by the Jamaica Regiment, called the *Compinsay*, to cross that stretch of the Caribbean, which usually took about three days in this flat bottomed boat offering the real possibility of a bad bout of sea sickness.

8
A Fusilier in Belize

The *Compinsay* regularly travelled the 1200 kilometres between Jamaica and Belize, taking supplies and mail, and the odd passenger like myself. It smelled strongly of diesel oil which I reflected, would not help anyone feeling sick, as I moved in with my kit to the cramped quarters below deck. I think I prayed for fine weather. The Gods smiled on me – with an uneventful journey across to Belize. Belize is situated on the mainland of Central America, at that time a colony, known as British Honduras. It is now an independent nation. Belize City is the capital.

We were able to move all the way into the harbour which probably explained the flat bottom of the *Compinsay*. I was pleased to get away from the ever present fumes, as I was greeted at the wharf by an MT member in a jeep, ready to drive me out to the camp, set in the middle-of-nowhere, some thirty kilometres out of town. The road to the camp was a ramshackle affair with only enough room for one vehicle at a time. With my kit aboard, I joined him in the front and we set off. The jeep moved through the outer streets of Belize, past wooden houses set on wooden supports above the ground, before hitting the narrow, poorly maintained road through tropical vegetation and many trees. This road, I would discover, was the one link between the camp and the city, and I would travel over it many times in the weeks ahead. I found the camp, set on a small plain, to be typical of all army camps with the guardroom with one small cell at the main entrance that I came to know well. The camp was surrounded by the same scenery as I had seen on the way; a complete self-supporting unit, with supplies brought from Jamaica by the *Compinsay*. Power for the place was supplied by its own generator, which needed to be started up each morning at approximately 5a.m. by the person unlucky enough to be detailed for the task. I had my turn at the joy of trying to start this contraption which could be extremely stubborn to start, if it wanted to be. To kick it into life required the turning over of a steel handle, very much in the manner of the vehicles of my youth with starting handles. In the coming of the dawn I would enter the shed where the generator was housed, turn on all that needed to be turned on, before gripping the handle in a determined bid to turn over the generator, and start it first time. There would be a chug-chug-chug before

Tom Stevens, in the uniform of the Royal Welch Fusiliers, Jamaica, with the white hackle, attached to the regimental badge on his beret. Tom sent the photograph to 'Mammy', his mother, Hetty.

the silence that usually followed my efforts, telling me my endeavours had been in vain. Attacking the handle with renewed vigour – palms sweaty despite the chill of the morning – I would restart the chug-chug-chug business, before, with a lot of luck, the chug would begin to quicken, building up to the sweet sound of a continuous hum, as the generator burst into life. Listening to the smooth running of the motor was a joy indeed. There were times when despite all attempts, the generator refused to wake up and help was needed by another person to kick over the engine, with double the energy and strength to turn the handle. I always hated having to seek such help and only did so when there was no alternative. If the generator ever did start first time, that was indeed a red letter day.

The camp had little in the form of entertainment, with a small NAAFI and no cinema facilities. It did have a large sports field where we played soccer. To seek our fun we needed to climb aboard the evening three-ton lorry for Belize City, where the evening was at our disposal until the return trip around 10.30 p.m.. The vehicle was always parked in a small yard close to the Police Station, so everyone knew the place of rendezvous. There was a small cinema, the only one, near the Police Station, and I have a vivid memory of seeing Mario Lanza in

The Great Caruso there. Many of the locals practised Spanish as their language, although the official, language was English. The films we watched usually retained their English soundtracks. The country's indigenous people had been Mayans, spreading from Guatemala into Mexico and Belize. The Maya mountains to the south of Belize, the home of the Mayan people for many centuries, run through both Guatemala and what was British Honduras.

From 1640 British woodcutters came to the coastal areas of Belize from Jamaica, where the great tropical rainforests of Honduras offered a bonanza to the adventurers. This coastal land really was the property of Spain but the Spanish did not show much interest, with Spain eventually giving over control to Britain. The logging thrived, with slaves coming from Africa mixing with the 'Black Caribs' (descendants of Africa and Caribbean ancestors).

In the mid-nineteenth century conflict in Mexico, to the north-west of British Honduras, drove Mexican refugees came to the northern part of Honduras. The boundary between Guatemala and the British colony had been decided in 1859, but Guatemala always disputed it, and was still doing so as the 'fifties rolled on. It was probably the main reason for us being stationed at Belize, with the Guatemalans often trying to create an 'incident' at the border.

For all that British Honduras was a remote colony, it received visits from the RAF, with the modern jet bomber, the Canberra, flying in, presumably to test its performance in tropical conditions. I heard that one Fusilier got himself into all kinds of bother guarding these aircraft. For reasons best known to himself he tossed a lighted cigarette butt far into the jet engines of one of these prized aircraft. I also saw modern vehicles there – it was in Belize that I caught sight of the first Land Rovers. The popular story of the time had Rover heading into financial disaster and needing to come up with something special to avoid going out of business. The Land Rover saved the company and apparently eventually made it a large profit – and now there are Land Rovers all over the world.

I found Belize to be infested with mosquitoes, probably the result of the swampy land on the coast. This coast runs from Mexico, along the full length of what is now Belize, down to Guatemala at the Gulf of Honduras. The coastal land is swampy and flat, where the great forests had once existed; to be found only inland in the mountains. The climate was humid and steamy for much of the time; the sky usually cloud-covered and grey. Gone was the blue-skied clarity of Jamaica. Instead we endured the steaming mists and rain of Belize. The snakes of Jamaica may have been wiped out but in Belize they were still a reality, even if not a real menace. We were certainly aware of them, as one drunken Fusilier was to find out on climbing into bed after a heavy night. The men of his hut had procured a length of thick rope from some source, which they curled around in a snake-like shape on his sheet, covered by blankets. Even although he was bemused with alcohol he assumed it was a large snake in the darkness, getting out of that bed quicker than he had ever got out of a bed before, drunk or sober.

I watched with interest, on one occasion, as a snake devoured a large frog alive, first by opening its jaws wide, before slowly, ever so slowly, drawing its body over the frog until it became simply a swollen lump protruding from the snake's insides. It did no seem to swallow the frog but its jaws seemed to be extremely flexible, and it eased its entire body over it, with the supple skin of the snake stretching to accommodate the prey. It was not such a large snake, and you would have bet money the feat was not feasible, or physically possible, to envelope a frog that size in such a way.

There were lots of scorpions in Belize as there were in Jamaica. A favourite party trick at the Belize camp was to place a live scorpion on a roadway, or some open ground, before pouring a circle of fuel around the intended victim. Putting a match to the petrol would send up a ring of flame around the scorpion which in an act of suicide would bring its tail over its body before taking itself out of the game, using the sting at the end of the tail to sting itself to death. We were such sweet boys.

There were, by all accounts, alligators in the rivers of British Honduras but I was never to see one. The only ones I ever did see was at British Guiana much later on when someone showed me a glass jar containing two or three perfectly formed specimens of a very young age. I was incredulous to realise these little harmless-looking creatures in the jar would develop into the ferocious, life-threatening monsters that alligators become eventually.

I have only thought about it since but one Sunday afternoon, feeling adventurous, I went exploring beyond the camp, taking with me a new camera I had bought. Fusilier Burkley decided to accompany me so, wearing soft green hats, known to us as 'hats, ridiculous', we tramped off into the unknown.

After following the river for some way we came to a couple of canoes resting on a bank. We decided to borrow one and go on a small expedition on the river; which we did, having the thrill of actually paddling along a river in Central America. We finally returned the canoe and explored further. But the point of this story comes down to our innocence in taking the river trip in such a flimsy craft, on a river that could easily have had alligators lurking in its waters. Not being proficient in canoe handling, we could have fallen into the river and then, who knows! When we are in our youth, strong in health and immortal in thought, we sometimes do things which years later we wonder about. As a sixteen-year-old I would go swimming in the mouth of the River Tawe, as it joined up with the waters of Swansea Bay. One of the things I did was to swim to a buoy, far out from the shore. On reaching the buoy I would climb aboard, sitting there on the bobbing contraption, enjoying the view of the shore, with the seagulls shrilling above. One attack of cramp on the outward or homeward swim would probably have finished me as I generally did this swim with no other person near. But that's youth for you!

I was given limited driving work because, as at Kingston, the old hands of the MT had the duties all sewn up. One of these duties included driving the recreational truck to the city in the evenings: affectionately known as the 'recce' truck. This vehicle would be a three-tonner and was driven by two MT mates on different nights. One of these men was known as Fusilier Daniels, a short, cheery type. The other driver went under the name of Fusilier Wilson, who was a dark, swarthy soldier, almost gypsy-like. These two men – both regulars with a lot of service – were long time friends, both sparking off one another, in a solid friendship. Both of these soldiers had served with the Royal Welch in Germany in pre-Jamaican days so they had come a long way together.

Wilson had the capacity to absorb alcohol as though his brain was wrapped in blotting paper, able to drive his truck back to the camp on dark or misty nights as though he had an inbuilt radar system. He would spend the evening drinking Bay rum, which in Belize was cheap and as popular lemonade. It had little if any effect on his driving ability. All of us had the most supreme confidence in this man, as he would negotiate the narrow road through the semi-jungle with us in the back of the vehicle, a little (or a lot) intoxicated, singing a variety of songs, clean and otherwise; our voices stabbing the silence of the night. I don't think Wilson would have fared too well in these days of breath testing but those were different times. To the best of my knowledge he was never involved in an accident, and always arrived on time at the Belize Police Station to drive us back to camp. Daniels, his mate, liked a drink also but was a different kettle of fish: full of zip and the quick come-back. Wilson was the silent type: even sober when drunk.

One miserable, overcast afternoon after a lot of heavy rain, with the road to the city slippery and puddle-filled; I was ordered to drive one of our officer's wives to Belize, using one of the jeeps for the trip. I was not getting enough driving on a consistent level and I must admit to feeling a little nervous with my passenger sitting so silently and stiff in the back of the vehicle as we set off past the dripping vegetation and rivulets of water at the side of, and across the road. The rain-laden sky was full of threat of further rain so the canvas roofing on the jeep was in place, in expectation. The road, apart from the water, had plenty of muddy soil streaked across it, very thick in some places. So with this mixture of water, oil and lots of soil I found the journey tricky, and I could feel the sweat trickle as I put in an intense concentration to negotiate the road. A pool of water turned out to be deeper than it appeared, causing the jeep to shudder at the impact, before regaining the initiative and passing on to firm, water-free, roadway. Some water had kicked up to the sides of the vehicle but it was not alarming and I remained perfectly dry. Not so the lady in the back though; she had been soaked. Though she said nothing to me, when she returned to the camp she reported me for careless driving. I was questioned about the incident, of course, and told my version to the orderly officer who gave me a grilling. He did not seem satisfied, however, and somehow I was sure I had not heard the end of the affair. My fears were to be justified the next day when I had the indignity of doing a driving test under a REME corporal. This gentleman took me some distance on the Belize City road before handing the vehicle over to me to drive and conduct emergency braking procedures, among other tests. I had no problems, with the corporal, seeming, and telling me he was satisfied. But I don't think it was what with the officer back at he camp wanted to hear, even if he had to accept the verdict. I can conclude that I was either thought of as incompetent, or I had got the lady wet by a deliberate act of bloody-mindedness; neither conclusions am I prepared to accept. Perhaps another vehicle, rather than an open jeep, would have been preferable for the journey, if you consider the conditions at the time. I was under a cloud of suspicion for some time, with my driving duties severely curtailed even less than before, spending boring hours of vehicle cleaning, and being a general helper around the MT yard.

One of our favourite haunts in Belize City was the dance hall, upstairs in the building opposite the Police Station. Here we would sit around drinking Bay rum or beer, watching the sweating dancers and making a serious study of the female anatomy. It was at this place, one fateful night, I saw the girl who would so affect my story in Belize, and also my life for months to come. She was small in stature but full in all the right places; with an Hispanic appearance showing a light golden skin, which enhanced her sparkling white teeth and the smile that tore at my heart.

9
Elvira

Her name was Elvira Margarita Cardona and she was eighteen or nineteen years of age. I was to discover that she lived in the centre of Belize City a few hundred yards from the dance hall where we first met. She had the most infectious laugh, which radiated a warmth and joy that captivated me. It offered the sensuous quality of music one can never tire of. In her clean, neat and colourful clothes and glistening black hair running down to her shoulders, she offered a contrast to the Jamaican women I had become accustomed to. She oozed sex, yet gave the impression of being removed from it. It was all a game of course. I was young in years and in the knowledge of how women reel a man in, a little at a time, before landing the fish she had always intended to catch. It was all about the chase in which the lead runner slows or races ahead but always intends to be caught at the finish line. I became completely besotted with this girl. Elvira had a good command of English but she used words with an economy that enhanced her mystery and the sexual mystique that surrounded her.

Elvira was at the dance hall with her elder sister Maria on the night of our first meeting. Maria was an attractive, mature, self-confident woman in her early to middle twenties. I later learned that she had married an Inniskilling Fusilier during his time in Belize and was awaiting permission to join him in Britain. I was always to have a good relationship with Maria, who had a good deal of common sense and personality, with a pretty shoulder for Elvira to lean on. I would meet Maria in future in Jamaica when she called on me on the way to join her husband. In the meantime I was interested in her sister. I can see now, of course, that I was probably never actually in love with this girl of Belize. It was mostly the chase for the unattainable, dressed in such an attractive package. I think a lot to do with it was having met what I considered to be a chaste girl after the prostitutes of Kingston.

At the dance at which we met I asked Elvira to join me on the floor. She agreed with a flashing smile. Holding her petite form in my arms she seemed to melt into them and become an extension of them, moving naturally to the music. She followed my steps perfectly with a sense of rhythm equal to mine. I have always considered myself to be good at dancing. I say that without being conceited.

Several of my cousins have been good at football, playing for local Swansea teams, but that skill seemed to have passed me by. But dancing came naturally. I was not so well versed in the copybook steps of the instructional manuals but found that I had a natural flair on the dance floor, able to improvise and create my own variations. I gained a reputation as a good dancer. I tried to draw some conversation from her but little was forthcoming. I did learn her name and told her mine. I couldn't tell if it registered on her thoughts which seemed some distance from my own eagerness. Elvira seemed preoccupied by the words to the tune the band played, singing for her own satisfaction rather than offering me any romantic hopes of a closer relationship to come.

The sisters went home together, leaving me to climb aboard the recce truck in the yard at the police station, my mind full of the evening and the dusky girl who had made it so memorable. I knew that I would not be able to push her away from my thoughts until the next opportunity to go back to the dance hall. I hoped that next time I would make a deeper impression. My fascination and even obsession with Elvira Margarita Cardona was well under way.

And so our relationship developed over the next few weeks. We mostly met at the same place, in the evenings, with Maria also part of the group at the table. I

Tom drawing Elvira from memory, after his return from British Honduras; the only surviving depiction of her.

would sip my drink with Elvira sitting on my lap in between the dances when we hurtled around the room, followed by the envious eyes of other men. I would be lost in Elvira's charms, often holding her closer than usual. I would place both arms around her tiny waist, in a very intimate way. This left her little option but to do the same, seemingly unsure and looking a little self-conscious. Matters progressed to the point where I was able to go out and meet Elvira, unhampered by the attractive but protective gaze of Maria. I was even allowed to call at the Cardonas' home, where I met her mother who, to the best of my knowledge, spoke only Spanish. Their home was not much more than a couple of poorly-lit rooms in a wooden building virtually alongside Belize City's main street. It was reached by a short passageway leading to the side of the structure, which seemed old, rickety and the worse for wear. Inside, I found the dwelling sparsely furnished, but clean, with the expected pictures of the Madonna and child adorning the poorly painted wooden walls. The place was shabby by British standards but this was Central America, not Swansea. I surmised that many in Belize lived like this or even worse. Memory has deserted me as to how the family got by but I suspect that Maria used her husband's allotment to put food on the table. I have no knowledge of the whereabouts of Mr. Cardona and I never asked.

Elvira and Maria's mother, mostly dressed in black, rattled out Spanish. Unused to hearing a foreign language, I was amazed that her daughters understood her. Maria took charge of the meeting leaving me with the impression eventually that I was not unwelcome in their home. I found the conversation strained but it was necessary if I was to make any progress with Elvira. Her mother's approval would be vital. It seemed that Elvira's mother had given me the nod, perhaps because of my dark complexion and black hair, but that was only a guess. At the end of each evening my last words to Elvira would always be, 'Shall I see you tomorrow?' and she usually nodded in answer.

So Elvira and I continued to see each other and the intensity of our relationship deepened. We went out to various events such as sports meetings or soccer games. We still visited the dance hall near her home, usually still with Maria. Elvira's sister was a very attractive woman who drew attention of many men at the dance hall. She maintained a discreet attitude to all advances and never put her marriage vows in jeopardy, spurning all advances, as far as I knew. This was one of the things I admired about her. I could not but conclude that her Inniskilling Fusilier must have been some man to evoke such loyalty and, above all, love. Across the intervening years I can now see that I was also perhaps a little in love with Maria, along with many others, I suspect.

But my daydreams centered on the lovely Elvira. I placed her on a pedestal, well nourished by the many romantic notions and Hollywood films that were such an important part of our lives. It was not realistic of course, but it was more my fault than Elvira's, even if she did have her own agenda of joining her lovely sister in marrying a soldier to enable her to leave the poverty and dullness of Belize. These were conclusions I was to form later. For the present I gave Elvira the status of a Spanish goddess. I didn't even attempt to have sex with her, thinking of our relationship as a great, unsoiled love affair. Although I had heard whispers of Elvira having had relationships with other soldiers I closed my ears and my mind to such disturbing thoughts. I was probably more in love with being in love with Elvira than with the actual facts of our relationship. Elvira herself made no secret of having gone out with other soldiers but she explained that there had been no serious involvement. I later found this to be untrue but at the time I was happy to believe what I wanted to believe. This was not so difficult to understand. I can see now a young soldier of twenty placed in the exotic world of Central America. He meets a slender, pretty Hispanic girl coming into womanhood, full of mystery, full of life. Take a lonely outpost of an army camp, miles from civilisation, even the civilisation offered by Belize City, and the possibility of being transferred back to Jamaica. Mix up these ingredients and it partly explains my madness and the suspension of reason that came with it. Above all, I was in love with the girl I thought Elvira was rather than the girl Elvira turned out to be.

Things soon reached a stage when I hated to miss seeing Elvira for a single night. Every opportunity I had I would be aboard the recce vehicle on my way to Belize City to spend some hours with Elvira, hating the need to return and be parted from her once more. Elvira did not seem to share my passion. She never seemed to be in the same mood on my visits, blowing hot and cold on our romance, making me in turn as happy as a sandboy and as miserable as a wet Monday in Manchester. If I was to say to Elvira 'Did you miss me?' I would never get a straight answer. She seemed to be the cold water tap and I the hot water. We would kiss but nothing much beyond that, although I was very conscious of her full shape beneath her dress, her young breasts straining beneath my ardent embraces. She was always dressed neatly, well scrubbed and smelling divine despite her humble circumstances and by now I was crazily in love with her. I began talking of us being married and spending our lives together in a long tale of joy and happiness. Even then I knew within that her mood swings and our disagreements did little to encourage such daydreaming. Apart from the differences in our race – of much greater importance then than now, especially in the Wales of fifty years ago – there was also Elvira's commitment to the Catholic faith. I knew that any children we had would be expected to follow her faith, also a problem in Chapel-going Wales. These difficulties, like others, did not appear insurmountable in the optimistic sunshine of youth and the headiness of romance. Let's face it, I was young and foolish – like many before me, and many after.

Elvira agreed to marry me and things became very serious. I applied for permission to marry but the major, the officer commanding the camp, refused my application. He had a wiser head on his shoulders than I. I guessed that as a result my time in Belize was probably limited and I would be sent back to Kingston soon. I decided to marry without permission, again, with the optimism of young love disregarding the forces ranged against us. I concluded that if I were able to find a minister prepared to marry us the army would be forced to accept the situation. I set about preparing a 'break-out' from the camp. I let one or two into the plan, one of whom was the driver of the vehicle going to Belize one Saturday morning. He stopped and allowed me to hide in the back and drove me to Belize to meet Elvira in the city, where we would try to find an official prepared to marry us. I committed serious offences: going absent without leave and disobeying orders even if I did not succeed in getting married but I was now obsessed with making Elvira my bride. Our union had become for me a beacon on a dark hillside.

Barry, a friend from Swansea living in married quarters, had agreed to help arrange things. With his wife he met Elvira, Maria and myself in Belize City. They put themselves to a lot of trouble, searching for a goldsmith who could make a ring at short notice. Barry was putting his own neck on the block in being a party to the clandestine wedding: he was subject to military discipline like me. But this did not deter him or his wife, who gave their best support and encouragement to our plan, sincerely believing in our commitment to each other. I met Barry several times in Swansea years later and we talked of that Saturday in Belize when a wedding would have taken place if we had found an official or a priest prepared to marry us. I can see now that it was probably beyond possibility that a ceremony could have been performed at such short notice, especially since I lacked permission. (I'd probably seen too many films.) Still, we tried just the same, going from one official to another. We had been told by the goldsmith we had found hunched over his work bench that a ring could be made but we held off the actual purchase until we knew that a wedding could take place. As the day wore on it became obvious that no wedding would be talking place. We said goodbye and thank you to Barry and his wife and they offered regrets and best wishes for whatever the future might hold for us. They were two good friends who acted with the best of motives even if, in the fullness of time, it became clear that they had been misguided in trying to help. Elvira and I reluctantly went back to her place.

It was not long before a truck pulled up at Elvira's house, a Fusiliers' truck. It carried four men, one of whom was the Company Sergeant Major known as CSM Davies (41). He was a tall, middle-aged man with an abundant greying moustache and a melodious Welsh lilt. Many had found to their cost that CSM Davies was not to be trusted. He had the reputation of being a sly fox who also hunted with the hounds if that would protect his own hindquarters. His fatherly tone and approach could lull you into a false security but he needed to be watched for he was a man with more than one face. The CSM told me that I was to be taken back to camp to face the music. I was allowed a brief moment to say goodbye to Elvira. I was sorry for both of us over how the day had turned out. I told her that it might be some time before I saw her again. It was obvious that one of the officials we had approached that day had got on to the camp and let the cat out of the bag probably for what they considered to be the best of reasons.

I found myself sitting in the back of the vehicle, well guarded, racing through the streets of Belize City and then out through the jungle and into the blackness of the night. Our headlights searched out the narrow road, for me leading to a heap of trouble. I suddenly felt tired from the emotion of the day and looked forward to sleep wherever I would find it that night.

Arriving at the camp I was greeted by a member of the guard with the words, 'Hello, Taff' – he was obviously English – 'you've got yourself in a spot of bother this time, haven't you?' I found that I was expected at the guard room and was placed in a not-so cosy cell, painted in white with a bed, mattress and bedding in one corner behind a metal door that would close on my freedom. There was only one cell in the building. The door had a small window quartered by bars. I could stand and look out at what was happening in the guard room while the guard commander could watch me, perhaps to ensure that I not try to harm myself. Things were going badly for me but they were not bad enough to drive me to suicide. I knew that I would sleep well that night because it had been a long day and I found myself exhausted. I lay in the darkness, allowing the events of the day to run through my thoughts, the light from without casting shadows on the cell walls. Tomorrow would be Sunday and I would have until Monday before I would face the consequences of my actions. I decided there and then to try to relax and make the most of the enforced rest.

Sleep overcame me that Saturday night as I wondered how Elvira was faring, in the darkness in Belize City and when I might see her again. I should have been a lot more anxious than I remember feeling at the time but the exhilaration of the day wrapped me in a cocoon that protected me from my true situation and what might befall me. I think I saw myself as a minor hero, prepared to sacrifice myself at the altar of love. I am sure that there were others who saw me as pretty stupid, not at all clever to fall for a pretty Spanish girl, even one as pretty as Elvira. Perhaps it was the romantic streak in the Welsh character but members of the guard regarded me as more of a celebrity than a criminal and I rather enjoyed the attention over that weekend.

I awoke feeling refreshed and uplifted by sleep, still borne along by a wave of unreality, though regretful that the wedding that had not occurred. Apart from visits to the toilet I spent the whole of Sunday in my cell. I was not treated harshly by the guard; rather the reverse. As evening closed on the camp, bringing with it a new guard, I was handed a letter by one of the incoming guard. It was from Elvira, written in surprisingly good English. I had no trouble understanding the serious accusations she made in describing what had taken place after I had been driven away that Saturday evening. Elvira wrote of how CSM Davies had given her a proposition: to be 'nice' to him in return for him to do what he could to minimize my troubles. Elvira said she had rejected his advances but felt that I should be aware of the man's behaviour. Although it was a very startling letter it did not shock me: it sat well with what I knew of his character. I felt sorry for Elvira, to end such a traumatic day being propositioned by this middle-aged lecher. But there was also another edge to the sword: this letter could be the life-belt that I needed to save me from the full force of army discipline. I was shrewd enough to realize that I had an ace up my sleeve that could give me some bargaining power. Having read the letter several times I put it in a safe place. In a perverse way I began to look forward to appearing before the detachment commander with my information.

Monday morning brought the order to appear before the OC, which I did with Elvira's letter in my pocket. There was the usual marching into the office at the quick time before being brought to attention before the officer seated at the table. The CSM was present, standing with his swagger stick tucked under his left arm, unaware of the time bomb that was about to explode away his veneer of humbug and hypocrisy. My rank, name and number were read out as a preface to the charges of going absent without leave and disobeying an order in attempting to arrange a marriage when such a marriage had not been permitted to proceed by

HM Forces. Ordinarily I could have expected weeks, perhaps months of detention in the Glass House (as soldiers called military prison), but I knew that I had information that would call into question the CSM's reputation and which might start a chain of events that the OC would not consider to be in his or the Royal Welch's interests. I had some leverage thanks to Elvira but I knew that I had to play my hand skillfully and not overplay it by being too vindictive toward my adversary standing so erect by the office window.

The OC gave me a lecture on how foolish I had been and how we soldiers were all ambassadors for Britain, and when we let ourselves down we also let down our regiment and our country, and so on ... with CSM Davies nodding in approval of this diatribe. He was stroking the ends of his moustache with his free hand in between nods, still grasping his stick smartly. I awaited my moment that eventually arrived as the lecture ended. Finally I was asked if I had anything to say before punishment was awarded, on the proviso that I was prepared to accept the officer's penalty on the matter. This was unwise to decline, because I would then go before the commanding officer of the battalion, in Jamaica, for judgment. This would have been a couple of extra black marks against me for turning down punishment from my company commander, and it would remove me from Belize.

Things did not go that way, for now was my chance to bring CSM Davies (41) down to join me in the mud. I spoke calmly and slowly, telling of the letter, explaining that I had it with me and describing how he had put the hard word on Elvira for sexual favours with a promise of leniency for me. There was, as they say, a pregnant pause. The OC collected himself to look briefly at the CSM and then quickly back to me before asking CSM Davies to answer my accusations. The man with the seductive Welsh voice now seemed to have lost it. He claimed that the whole story was a fantasy on Elvira's part, the trumped up allegations an obvious ploy to save my bacon. I now wonder whether he was right, but at the time I believed Elvira and in spite of everything I still believe her. I knew that my words had struck home with the two other men in the room, for different reasons. It added up to a very useful answer to my prayers and gave me some breathing space.

The OC did not accept the letter as evidence and I was marched outside to await his deliberations as he and the CSM battled it out. The silly love-sick Fusilier had given them something to think about. He had poured a bucket of manure over the proceedings and they needed to find a way of avoiding the smell. They found a way. I was brought back in for my punishment. I was told that I would be returned to the MT in Kingston shortly and that that would be the end of the affair: naturally marriage to Elvira was out of the question. Although I was not happy to farewell Elvira I had the good sense to understand how lucky I had been in all other ways, considering the charges laid against me. I had no choice but to accept the verdict, with the thought of finding a way back to Belize beginning to buzz around in my mind even as I did so. There had to be a way somehow. I really did believe that there was, in the crazy optimism of youth when you are convinced that all is possible. In reality, returning to Belize from Jamaica would have been impossible and deep inside I knew it.

I had my full freedom restored, even being allowed to go into Belize City while arrangements were made for my return to Jamaica. I talked to Elvira, trying to convince her that all was not lost between us but now I felt doubts closing in as the energy of recent events began to wind down and a little common sense slowly replaced it. I was to return to Kingston on the *Compinsay* when it arrived in a few days time. Elvira and I made good use of the little time we had, finding a real closeness, a relief from the hot and cold relationship we had had, without the wild mood swings that had always been such a worrying feature of it for me. Elvira seemed very genuine in her feelings for me, saying how much she would miss me. We wasted no time now in silly disputes, each showing the other consideration and tenderness as the days quickly passed.

On my very last night in Belize Elvira and I walked in a loving embrace to an old wooden wharf at the water's edge, looking out over a calm, moonlit sea. We had the rotting wharf to ourselves, the water visible through the gaps between the planks, with the slap-slap of the waves breaking the silence. The moon was bright and full, looking down on us as we sat and then lay on the wharf, locked in an ardent embrace. We remained there for a long time, perhaps a couple of hours, kissing, talking, reflecting, projecting the future that would begin when my ship sailed away. It was not a sexual adventure: somehow that would have tarnished the night. We were content to know closeness of a kind stopping short of inter-course – I wanted to reserve that for a wonderful reunion when that came. Young people of today may read that in amazement. There was a sadness, a bitter-sweet feeling deep within as I was now closer to Elvira (and I felt that she was closer to me) than at any time since we had met about months before. For that brief, balmy evening we clung to emotions, with little time for petty squabbles, enjoying each in other what was really important. We sat, loved and talked in the Belize moon-light, with no other human to spoil the spell. But time always wins in the end and if I wanted to catch the truck and avoid further difficulties we had to leave this magic spot. I had said my goodbye to Maria earlier that evening. All that remained was a last agonizing farewell to Elvira. As things turned out it would be final in every way except for one incident aboard ship en route back to Britain.

My time in Belize had been short but memorable, very much like the B-movies I enjoyed so much. As I sat in the darkness with the truck speeding through the mosquito-ridden jungle I pondered on what might befall me after I had left the colony. It was not very inspiring but I knew that I would have to make the best of things, keeping as my goal being reunited with Elvira. There was not much sleep for me back at camp. The morning came, bringing dark shadows under my eyes and a tiredness of body and mind. I wished that I could climb out of my skin and find a restful spot and drift away in dreams to a place where I would find Elvira, a much more appealing vision than the diesel-engined ship I would soon board. Soon I was once more passing through the streets of Belize City, close to Elvira's tiny home. I sat with full kit beside me in the back of the truck heading for the wharf. I had the company of a Fusilier John Davies who was also returning to battalion headquarters. I have no knowledge of why he was returning to Kingston but it was certainly not the result of a mad romantic escapade.

Soon we sailed away from the wharf, through the shallow water leading to the Caribbean Sea, Belize's shoreline receded as I stood at the *Compinsay's* side, silently farewelling an unseen figure and a place which had given me such a mixture of emotions. The water around us began to swell as the sky turned an ominous grey. It matched my mood as I finally went below to begin a horrific bout of sea-sickness which was to last the entire voyage.

I soon had my head in a bunk, listening to the sickening throb-throb of the ship's engine searing into my tired brain, the heaving motion of the ship taking my stomach up to somewhere and leaving it there. I was wishing I was anywhere but in that flat-bottomed prison. I saw through suffering eyes my companion was in a similar condition, stretching his agonized frame on his bed before doubling up to try to gain relief in the foetal position. For hours I lay suspended in a vacuum of misery, wondering how the crew could stay on their feet, let alone perform their duties. John Davies and I drifted in and out of a half-sleep of suffering, too ill to care about food, passing through waves of nausea. It felt as if we would sail forever in the torture of the swollen sea, grey sky taken over by huge black clouds hanging low over the ship. Night and day became one, lost in a blur of a continuous squirm in the gut and always the thump-thump of that engine. We had been given a cooking stove and once brewed up some corned beef stew with hard biscuits. At first the food was welcome, its warmth bringing a new lease of life. But it soon made us want to vomit and we left the meal to return to our bunks. The theory was that it was better to eat something rather than to retch. We wanted to eat, even felt hungry, but after a few morsels it would be back to the bunk. All the stories we'd heard of sea-sickness on the *Compinsay* came true. All colour drained from our tanned faces and we remained on our bunks, huddled up as if in the womb, for the entire voyage across the Caribbean.

At last the voyage ended as we brushed the wharf at Kingston, our crew making fast the ship, probably, like us, glad the voyage was over. The brilliant sun stabbed our eyes as we staggered up onto the wharf, pulling our kit with us. Even though the motion of the boat was now a gentle one I was still responding to the past three days with the *Compinsay* rising and falling fiercely in my mind. These sensations would remain with me for several hours. We found a vehicle waiting to take us to Up Park camp and we were soon negotiating the familiar hectic streets of Kingston before reaching the camp and the MT section in particular.

I found most people already aware of my exploits in Belize, eager to know my side of the affair and what my plans might be. I settled down in the MT, writing to Elvira regularly. It was always a red-letter day when I heard from Belize. I regarded these letters as milestones on my road to being reunited with Elvira. I remember doing a large drawing of her, working in colour from a photograph of her standing by a window, with a small table on which is a vase of flowers. Her photograph and the drawing have long been destroyed, though she can be glimpsed in a photograph of me with a drawing of her. Everything I did, everywhere I went, Elvira was always with me, in a bitter-sweet kind of self-torture. I went out, but it was all superficial – my mind was in Belize, far from my body. The days slowly passed, turning into weeks and months, with no real prospect of solving the problem of how we might meet again. Then Elvira's letters began to drop off and those that arrived seemed detached and distant. Then they stopped altogether. Things became clearer when a mate returned to the MT from Belize. He told me that I deserved to know that Elvira was seeing another soldier there. He was sorry to bring such tidings. The news hit me hard, even though I had half-expected it, and it was a little while before I came to terms with it. I never again wrote to her, and I never heard from her again. I can see now that there was no chance that the army would have sent me back to Belize, and I could never have married Elvira as a serving soldier. Perhaps Elvira was even more realistic than I was. In time I heard that she had married her new admirer, a man also in the Royal Welch Fusiliers, a full corporal. It is probable that Elvira's agenda had been to marry a military man, as her sister had done, to find a way out of Belize.

Perhaps we were never really in love. We were two people from very different cultures who had been brought together by an eruption of feelings, part love, part expediency, all in the setting of Belize. I am convinced that at the very end of our affair Elvira had begun to love me, even if it had begun as more of a business proposition for her. Wherever she is today I wish her true happiness and I hope she has had a good life. I do not regret one minute of the time I spent with her, the years having taken away all hostility.

Some time later Elvira's sister Maria suddenly turned up one afternoon at Up Park camp with another woman from Belize. Outside my barrack room, in the late afternoon glow of the Jamaican sun, we stood chatting. Maria told me that she and her friend (another Inniskilling bride) were at last on their way to join their husbands in Britain. Maria looked very beautiful and quite radiant. She told me that things between Elvira and I could have worked out if only I could have returned to Belize but I was not convinced. I was hurt that she had found someone else so soon. Maria said that I looked healthy, having put on weight since she had last seen me. Jamaica was good for me, she said, because I appeared so relaxed. I guessed that it was probably because I was getting enough sleep rather than racing into Belize at every opportunity, spending the nights tossing and turning thinking of our often turbulent relationship. I had to conclude that Elvira had been like a drug for me. Now the habit had been broken, giving me a new lease of life.

For a long time I did not feel good about Elvira and her fickle love but time heals. Many years later in Swansea I was told that Elvira's marriage had broken up. She was then said to have gone 'on the game' somewhere in Kent. This may not have been true: I had no way of knowing, but I prefer not to think of her in that situation. I think only of the pretty, dainty young thing she was that last night we spent together in the moonlight. For me she does not age. Even if I live to be a hundred she will never be any older than she was that night, when we were young and I was in love.

10

Kingston and the de Baroviers

So it was soldiering in Kingston once more. I now became the MT clerk, a job that involved planning and setting up the duty roster for the battalion's motor transport for the day ahead. The battalion needed vehicles for a whole range of duties: taking equipment or meals to the rifle range, for example, collecting film from a cinema in Kingston for showing at the camp. A truck was required for the use of the duty officer of the day, on call for his use. The MT clerk's skill lay in matching the vehicles and drivers available to cover the needs of the battalion. Apart from the driving schedule the MT clerk was responsible for the Fire Piquet. Each day these men would report to the MT office. After working hours they were allowed to sit about reading, playing cards (not for money, officially), listening to the radio or writing, though forbidden from leaving the vicinity. The Fire Piquet had to sleep at the MT office and provide a guard for the MT buildings, trucks and petrol and oil stores. It was an irksome rather than hard chore and most men avoided it if they could because they were restricted to the camp. The task of selecting the Fire Piquet was in the MT clerk's hands using a rota to ensure that each man did his share of duty. There were times when the job was exacting. The clerk had to keep everyone on side while picking men for unwelcome jobs. Often a soldier was prepared to swap a Fire Piquet with someone else and the arrangement had to go through me. I learned to type on an old Remington in the office, very slowly, tapping the keys with two fingers as the daily schedule had to appear typewritten on the MT notice board. How this job fell into my hands I have no recollection but it came my way anyway. Perhaps they thought I was a bit bookish – I always had a book in my hand – perhaps it was a job given to a newcomer.

The sour Captain Davies – no relation to CSM Davies, of course – had left the job of running the MT Section. He had been replaced by the tall and much more popular Captain Jones. He was much more relaxed in his approach. As long as the MT operated on an even keel he kept a low profile, sitting in his office for a few hours each day before shooting off, probably to the Officers' Mess, unseen until the following morning. With work busy, and sometimes hectic, my regrets about what might have been with Elvira receded from my thoughts and I became content with life again. I was free to enjoy the fleshpots of the capital and to explore such historic places as Port Royal when I wanted some culture.

Port Royal stood at the end of a narrow isthmus jutting out into Kingston harbour. The road to Port Royal was a narrow one that ran past Palisadoes Airport (now Norman Manley International Airport, named after one of Jamaica's founding politicians). The airport's runway extended into the sea. During my time in Jamaica – it could have been 1952 – a passenger plane left the runway and crashed into the sea. I heard the macabre story that divers had gone down to find dead passengers still strapped into their seats. The Palisadoes road featured in the James Bond film, *Dr. No*. I recognized the road immediately when I saw the film in Wales a decade later.

Much of the old town of Port Royal also stood in a watery grave, lost forever in the earthquake of 1692, with the loss of two thousand lives. It had been the head-quarters of the pirates and ruffians of the Caribbean, where they had caroused with rum and wenches before plundering treasure ships and performing the most cruel and vile acts and giving no quarter. The story goes that Port Royal became such a wicked den of vice and debauchery with men like Henry Morgan and William Teach ('Blackbeard') sailing the Spanish Main that God brought the earthquake on to sink the sinful city beneath the sea. I was told at the time a boat passing over the lost city gives a view of walls and buildings of the pirate strong-hold, still sitting beneath the waves, if the water is clear enough. (I never saw this phenomenon for myself.) Captain Morgan – a Welshman – later in his life went on to become respectable as governor of Jamaica with a title to go with it. At what remained of Port Royal stood Fort Charles, in some decay, but still very much retaining the atmosphere of the days of cannon and cutlass. An ancient cannon still stood, pointing out to sea, where once the galleons and pirate ships may have graced the horizon. At the fort a plaque, set in the stone walls, stated the following that 'In this place dwelt Horatio Nelson. You who walk in his footsteps, Remember his glory...'

A yarn doing the rounds at our time on Jamaica told of a man being buried alive into the stonework of Fort Charles many years past and appearing as a ghost on any photograph taken of that spot, complete with a sailor's beard, full and pointed underneath the chin. The simple explanation to this spectre was very mundane. A photograph of the entrance to Fort Charles, near the man's horrible burial, showed an arrangement of stones in different textures, which appeared on a black and white photo as the figure of a man from long ago complete with ruffled material around his neck, as if from the days of Elizabeth I. It made a good story even if it only came down to the shapes and shades of the stone bringing about the illusion. Port Royal and Fort Charles breathed history: with the boisterous voices of long-ago seamen lost on the gentle breeze that rustled the palm trees. One day I stood on the ramparts of the fortifications looking out on a slightly choppy harbour. The fort was deserted apart from our party of three or four that particular day, walking indeed on the slabs of stone on which the great admiral had once stood, perhaps holding his eye glass to survey the sea. What stories the silent old walls could tell of men and treasure, loss and violence, of the skull and crossbones flying from masts of ships sailing the Caribbean in search of plunder, and of that terrible day in 1692 when the disaster struck, taking much of Port Royal below the sea. I could sense the past: heavy in the air: closing in on me, creating a feeling of awe on being at this place of buccaneers, death and England's history.

So much for the past: in the present, films were very important to us. Kingston had a mixture of open air and conventional cinemas, but most were covered. In the open-air cinemas it was possible to view the films beneath a bright mantle of stars on balmy Jamaican evenings, with many of the local ladies dressed in cool, colourful dresses and long gloves, some in stylish hats too: making an evening at the cinema a Jamaican social event.

Up Park camp was situated near a part of Kingston known, for no good reason I knew of, as the Spot, where most things were available without going into the city proper. At the Spot stood 'Uncle's': a well-organised, clean restaurant run by Jamaicans of Chinese origin. The food was memorable and at a price we soldiers could afford. We often celebrated pay night with a large steak surrounded by tasty French fries and washed down with a couple of ice cold 'Red Stripe' beers. Just a little way from 'Uncle's' was the 'Silver Slipper', a dance hall on its upper storey with music supplied by a juke box complemented by a drinking area, with bar at ground level. The 'Slipper' was a favourite watering hole for Fusiliers out for a night at the Spot. So far as dancing is concerned, the place did nothing to attract many women, falling between two stools, in that it was too classy for the prostitute type and not good enough, partly through location, for more respect-able women. Most of us spent time there sitting at table, sipping a beer, playing a popular tune of the day on the jukebox, and looking around at a very large and empty dance floor. We heard the story at the time of how the film star Errol Flynn had been thrown out of the 'Slipper' when worse for drink on one of his legendary binges. The 'Slipper' was a couple of hundred yards or so from the very popular and fully enclosed Carib cinema: probably Kingston's finest at that time. It was here that the latest film releases were shown and were patronised by the cream of Jamaica's – so-called – top people, filtering down to members of the Royal Welch Fusiliers and those of the public rich enough to afford admission and prepared to break free of the places mostly frequented by the lower orders. Like places everywhere Jamaica had its own class structure. It seemed that the hierarchy was based on colour, but not just between blacks and whites but between degrees of blackness, with darker people occupying a lower level. Each kept usually to its own which in Kingston included patrons of the cinemas. At cinema and dance places we were able to meet some of Kingston's more respectable inhabitants and it was in this way I met the de Baroviers.

And so one Saturday afternoon I came to meet the two de Barovier sisters, sitting in the seats in front of Bert Yale and myself at the Carib Cinema. Bert was an Englishman on the REME staff at the MT, coming from the north of England. I had struck up a friendship with the lance-corporal, mostly as a pal to go to the pictures with. I think the conversation began by commenting on the film, but that is not really important. By the end of the afternoon we were chatting away on several topics. We lingered in the foyer after the show, the four of us engrossed in chit-chat. They introduced themselves as Marietta and Lisetta de Barovier, whom we would discover later, were the two daughters of a Countess, Madame de Barovier, as she was known. If she really was a Countess I do not know but by all accounts she had once been married to an Italian Count and although divorced, still retained the title. Marietta was the tall one, with very long hair to her shoulders: hair that appeared European in spite of her mother who was very dark and of African descent. Marietta had a teasing manner with a fair supply of sex appeal, without being a great beauty. Her long legs were an attractive feature, and she possessed a great deal of energy, running around on them playing a great deal of tennis. Marietta spoke loudly, with something of an inane laugh, as she tossed her long, almost ginger, hair around her shoulders when she talked. I never really got close to Marietta – her brash style held no appeal for me.

Lisetta was the older of the two, more sedate and studious, with plainer looks. She was less European-looking than her sibling, with much of her mother's part African colour, with tight and frizzy hair close to her scalp. She was the one to talk to on serious issues, with Marietta the nonsense queen. I found Lisetta more to my liking and we had a sound platonic friendship.

Bert and I were given an open invitation to call at the de Baroviers' home at Halfway Tree for drinks. This was a better class of area near to the Spot, in a nice

Lisetta de Barovier and Tom's friend Bert Yale, Kingston, 1953.

residential group of fine houses, after passing through the commercial sites of the Spot, surrounded by green lawns and leafy trees. The girls had set down instructions for Bert and I to find the place that we followed one day, having decided to take up her offer. The area was within walking distance from the camp, so one Saturday or Sunday we set off to Halfway Tree, dressed in casual civilian clothes, hoping our invitation had been a sincere one and we would be made welcome.

The home was fairly large, set in a spacious, flower-laden garden, through which a gravel driveway twisted its way to the imposing front entrance which featured a wooden archway set over the front double doors. A good looking black car stood outside shining in the sunshine. (It seemed to me to be an English model, a Morris or an Austin, a sign that the de Baroviers were certainly not poor.)

We were made welcome with a genuine grace, offered drinks of rum and coke and taken into a large room that was well and nicely furnished. A painting dominated the wall before me, as I sat at the edge of my lounge chair, still not relaxed as yet in the company of the Countess, whom we were meeting for the first time.

Tom and his friend Bert Yale, in sports shirts and bags relaxing at the de Baroviers one Sunday morning.

The colourful painting showed the de Barovier sisters with their mother facing the artist, but all their subjects had only dark shadows where the eyes should have been. The artist, for a reason that has now deserted me, had expressed himself by deliberately leaving out these windows on the soul but it was still easy to recognise the people concerned. I was later to hear more on this strange artist the de Baroviers' had known for a period, when he had spent time on the island on his way around the word, as he had told them before one day shutting himself in a room eventually, to paint the masterpieces he would produce. Today I wonder what became of his ambitions (and his paintings), but I have no way of knowing, with his name long ago lost on the winds of memory. I can remember how the painting had been one of broad brushwork, nothing fussy, and how the figures were surrounded by green, exotic plants and palms.

At the time I was fascinated by the painting and tales of its creator, thoughts of which were among my beginnings of a real interest in art, which I was to develop later in life as a practising artist. As I studied the work, Bert chatted to

Marietta. She talked loudly and played with her long hair, shaking the ice blocks in her drink. Lisetta was present, sitting quietly, a pleasant smile on her lips, content to sit in on the conversation. The Countess de Barovier was short, plump and possessed a cheerful, commanding personality. She liked to take charge of company, very often doing this by sitting at the piano, running her fingers along the keys, singing a tune from a musical comedy, urging everyone to join in the chorus. The lady (it turned out) had a musical background, interested in anything of that nature, always prepared to be involved in theatrical productions, be they small or otherwise. She had a good voice able to reach the high notes with ease and spent much time at the piano, playing the sheet music that completely and heavily covered the top of it. The Countess was involved with an organisation called the International Club, formed to foster good relations with the peoples of the world, collecting funds to keep the Club financial by cabarets, concerts, and dinner parties. Perhaps this interest in nationalities was one of the reasons Bert and I were made welcome at the de Barovier home with complete acceptance, even though we represented the army of a dominating country; despite an awareness things were moving to an inevitable change.

Our visit passed quickly, the first of many, with Bert and I strolling back to camp talking of our impressions, pleased with the way things had progressed since first meeting the two sisters, in getting involved with community life as opposed to the low life of the brothels for a change. We were to discover the Countess had a grown son living at home, a technician with Radio Jamaica who kept himself to himself, shut off in his room containing a collection of radio gadgets, doing whatever he did with them. Bert and I were to see very little of this man. We heard him drive up to the house or drive away, and heard his footsteps as he moved around in his room, but barely saw him. When we first met the de Baroviers they seemed to live this leisured life with few financial worries but they became poorer through a crisis of some kind, leading them to restrict things such as evening drinks to Bert and I. Some months later they moved to a smaller home nearer to our camp. I never knew what was behind the financial crisis but one was able to see the gradual decline in their prosperity. Bert and I kept our relationship with the two sisters on a purely platonic level (so far as I was able to tell), with Bert and Marietta striking up their own bond of friendship that continued on some level after I had moved on and left the scene. Lisetta and I too had our brand of relationship as very good friends with a general interest in most things right up to the time of her leaving the island to attend Oxford University. Perhaps supporting Lisetta at this famous place of learning may have been one of the contributing factors in the family's financial fortunes running downhill. Never at any time did anything other than friendship pass between Lisetta and myself, with no physical attraction on my part getting in the way of things. Her attraction to me lay only in her serene demeanor, and interest in other things apart from the things that motivated Marietta, who got immediately bored when events took too serious a turn. I reached an understanding with Lisetta that I did not even have with Bert who, apart from his very sound knowledge of vehicles, also had a limited outlook on most things. Marietta and I did not spark too well, even though I must confess her lithe body with the long, tanned legs did excite me. We were, it seems, never on the same wavelength, and I often found her biting, sarcastic wit somewhat hurtful.

My employment as MT clerk had become more or less a permanent one. Usually the job carried the rank of lance-corporal, offering the protection of some authority when dealing with the problems of the daily roster. One of the MT corporals suggested my promotion to Captain Jones, and in due course this happened, becoming acting unpaid lance-corporal until qualifying for the fully paid variety over a period of some weeks. When that did come about I found the extra pay very acceptable.

Bert (who was also a one-stripe wonder) and I became regulars at the home of the de Baroviers': sitting on the patio on warm, balmy evenings, sipping at our drinks, listening to Madame play the piano or engaged in intense conversation as we relaxed in a world far away from army discipline. On occasions Bert and I would escort the two girls to the cinema, once joined by Madame, and one time the five of us went to the Glass Bucket night club which was a popular place to go dancing with a real live band. Before we left the de Barovier household Madame offered me the loan of a smart white dinner jacket. Trying it on, it transformed my image, even if too long in the sleeves, and some surplus material hanging around my back. I became Humphrey Bogart in 'Casablanca' in my mind as I preened before a long mirror but I probably looked like some dork wearing a dinner jacket that was too big for him. Against my better judgment I found myself wanting to wear it, but I was able to tell that Marietta was not impressed by it, and I nearly chickened out. Still, I took my thin body and the beautifully cut jacket hanging on my sparse frame, along to the Bucket for an evening of kicking up a storm on the intimate, circular wooden dance floor beneath the stars, shining as bright as you could imagine, twinkling in a clear topical night. Tables, each with their own table lamp, were scattered around the floor, as waiters hovered in the shadows of the palms, acting as a backdrop to the tables as they attended to every need of the patrons. These waiters were smartly dressed in their high cut dinner jackets of spotless white, contrasted with their dark skins. With the best of the nightclub being exposed to the elements, I wondered on the possible protection from rain for the wonderfully smooth floor. I guessed they probably had covering ready to pull over it in the event of a downpour. At one edge of the floor, playing on a raised stage, the band did an excellent job with a slow fox-trot, being equally as good with a wild samba or a calypso as I was soon to discover. Before each player stood a wooden rectangular shield bearing the initials of the band. Already my feet were itching to hit the floor, and I asked Lisetta if she would do me the honour. As I attempted to dazzle the onlookers at the tables with my ballroom prowess I was able to spot Bert and Marietta sedately moving out onto the floor making no attempt to try anything venturesome. Lisetta tried patiently to follow my ambitious steps which sometimes ended in a scuffle of feet when things did not succeed in coming off. At times I noticed Marietta glance in our direction in a haughty way, probably unimpressed with my exhibitionism but I didn't let it stick. I felt rather dashing in my dinner jacket. It was obvious that Marietta was far more at home on a tennis court than on the floor of the Glass Bucket: a look of boredom covered her face.

I would visit the night club on several occasions over time, the most memorable being on New Year's Eve 1953. By that time, as you will read, I had passed on beyond the de Baroviers and was deep in a relationship with a woman called Marcia. Not far from our table sat Bert with Marietta, and I could not help but feel good to have them see Marcia in my company, radiant and attractive. I stopped by them to say a few words of small talk during the course of the evening; which was a celebration to welcome in 1954 but carried a tinge of regret for me in that I would be leaving Jamaica in the coming March. The New Year came in to the usual razzmatazz of singing and cheering but Marcia and I, although we celebrated, felt our joy muted by the knowledge of our parting to come. I looked across at Bert and Marietta to see them looking at us: making me proud to hold Marcia close. But this lay in the future. For the present Bert and I were enjoying the friendship and the hospitality of the de Baroviers, spending up to four or five nights a week at their home or escorting the two sisters to various places. Madame introduced us to her world of beautiful people, charity functions, and the International Club meetings and cabarets.

My time in Jamaica expanded my horizons in many ways, and the de Baroviers played a great part in that expansion.

11

Cadre days

In February 1953 we received shocking news. A plane carrying members of the Royal Welch Fusiliers, including wives and children, had gone down into the Atlantic, somewhere near Newfoundland. No trace of the plane or its passengers and crew was ever found. An 'air trooping service' had been introduced, bringing Britain and Jamaica much closer. It made exchanges of personnel simpler and quicker than by sea. Men coming to the end of their National Service could be returned to Britain, and their replacements could be sent out from the Welsh training depot at Brecon without having to wait for larger and slower ships. The air trooping service had proved popular with everyone in the battalion, especially married couples, with wives and children able to join us or return to Britain much more easily. If my memory serves it was about the twentieth flight to reach us from Britain when disaster struck. I record the names of those lost, names that will not mean much to most people so many years on, but in honour of a sad loss to the small regimental family that was the Royal Welch Fusiliers.

David Barker
Horace James Bayliss
Leslie Ann Bayliss
Doris Edith Bayliss
Elizabeth Anna Busst
Jasper Vincent Gwyn Busst
Colin James Busst
Trevor Gwynn Busst
William Aubrey James
Violet Laura James
Sydney Glaze
Della Platt
Donald Owen Platt
Dale Tierney
Linda Tierney

Margaret Tierney
Bernard Michael Vaughan
Moira Evelyn Vaughan

The effect of this disaster on the battalion was profound, with the suddenness and unexplained mystery of the accident adding to the sadness. The air trooping service was suspended. National Servicemen due for release having to be patient: to their credit they were. They understood that their need was much less important than the loss of the families affected by the crash. I later composed a short elegy for those who were lost on their way to join the battalion:

The waters cover you
But do not drown your memory
Washed up forever on the sands of time.

*   *   *

Around this time an NCOs' cadre – a training course for aspiring non-commissioned officers – was to commence at Newcastle. The MT Section was asked to supply one NCO. I volunteered to be the one, to the howls of those who thought that playing at soldiers in the Blue Mountains came a very poor second to the cushy number of being MT clerk. Captain Jones had returned to Britain on a course, to be replaced by a young National Service officer, Second Lieutenant Knight. Things were going on smoothly in the Section, but I had become a little weary of the constant juggling of MT duties and felt that I had something to prove. Having been made a lance-corporal on the strength of my position as MT clerk I felt that in some ways my promotion was bogus. By going on the cadre I felt that I would satisfy myself at least that I was worthy of the stripe. This was a noble but probably stupid thought: I should have known by now never to volunteer for anything in the Army. By volunteering I am sure there were glad faces on the MT strength who were pleased I was going in their place.

Soon after I found myself climbing aboard a vehicle bound for Newcastle. In all there were twenty-four of us, a mixture of full corporals and lance-corporals. Everything looked familiar as we rounded the final bend in the road and groaned up the hill towards Newcastle camp. For the next six weeks I was going to earn my soldier's pay, I thought as we rolled onto Newcastle's spacious square. I was to be proved right but was still glad to have taken part.

Tom (with hat and scarf) with his mates – a sign of the comradeship he enjoyed in the army.

The cadre covered a range of military training. There would be plenty of drill on the square and tests of each man's ability to take drill. We took it in turns. One of us would stand alone, shouting out commands while the rest of the squad complied. The course emphasised weapons training, together with much route marching and other fitness routines. We spent much time on the rifle range, giving us time to fire the Lee-Enfield again and also the Bren and Sten guns. At the end of the course we would have to sit a written examination. Of course, I was familiar with the camp's layout but other members of the cadre may not have been. I was under some disadvantage in that I had not done any real soldiering for some time, having been in semi-retirement as MT clerk. Many of my companions had come directly from the rifle companies where playing soldiers was the name of the game. Some, if not all, had been promoted on the strength of their soldierly qualities, so I knew that I would have to dig deep to come up to let alone pass, their level. But being back in the clear, cool air of Newcastle with a goal to achieve away from the hum drum days at the MT I felt a confidence within. I would soon be fighting fit again, marching and running around the mountainside, in spite of the many cigarettes I smoked in those days. (It would be another fifteen years before I would give them up.) But it takes many cigarettes to break down the defences of early manhood, and in those cadre days I was as fit as I would ever be in my life.

In the meantime there was also plenty of pain, plenty of sweat and plenty of abuse from the senior NCOs in charge. We visited the camp's miniature rifle range, lying down in the enclosure, shooting at small targets placed on the steep bank ahead of us. (The camp was on mountainside and did not lend itself to a full size rifle range.) A track passed in front of the targets, so great care had to be taken that no one was near when firing was under way. I found the Lee-Enfield heavy to hold and fierce to fire. From war films and westerns you might think that a rifle was easy to aim and shoot: it wasn't. Firing the Lee-Enfield was all about holding the rifle correctly, with a lot to do with breathing before easing the trigger rather than just pulling it. Being only slightly built then, the force of the recoil would kick into my shoulder. By strapping the thick gauze pad from a field dressing beneath my shirt I was able to dull much of the shock. With the pad in place I could get by reasonably well even if I was not the best shot of the cadre.

There was much marching around the big square where the two old cannons still stood guard. When my turn to take drill came around I found that shouting commands was not easy because I did not have a powerful voice compared to some. After these sessions I would have a sore throat with the effort of trying to throw my voice in a commanding way. Those who had deep voices and could project the sound up from their stomachs were fortunate. But with the course being so varied everyone had a chance to shine at something. I surprised myself one day while doing an exercise dressed in full battle order and carrying a rifle. The task involved us marching away from the camp before turning back to it, continuing to the rifle range before firing off at a target. The full distance we had to cover was about thirteen kilometres and it had to be covered within a certain time. Hitting the target was not going to be easy because by that time we would be breathing heavily, running in the heat of the day with heavy steel helmets jumping around on our heads.

The weather that day was hot and sunny. I could feel the streams of sweat trickle down my face and back as we trudged along the road, layered with a thin, white dust. The men had broken into small packs as the test progressed and I realized that I would have to break free of the group I was with and catch the front runners if I was to have any chance of qualifying. Many had decided that it was sufficient simply to finish the course in whatever time it took at the best speed they could manage. I forged out ahead of the pack, leaving the stragglers behind. I felt somewhat uneasy breaking away from the group, fearing that they might think that I was trying too hard to be a hero. The dust had settled on my skin, carried into my shirt by the rivulets of sweat. The mixture of sweat and grime strangely gave me an odd sensual pleasure as I felt it spread over my chest. The material of my shirt beneath my arms was soaked in big patches: I could even smell the salt. But I pushed on, passing one or two others as I searched for the leaders. By this time I had reached the outskirts of the camp and felt a renewed energy pushing me on to my limit. The worst was over I knew, having arrived at a level where the rocky road and the heat did not register on my mind.

As I entered the camp, running across the square, I could see two of the course sergeants sitting on the steep incline of the buildings, noting the cadre as they passed. I steeled myself to appear more relaxed than I felt and strode out at a faster pace. The two sergeants looked at my efforts with curiosity, sitting in the sun in their comfortable seats outside the Sergeants' Mess with clipboards, marking our progress. Looking back I could see a small group of runners coming around one of the last bends in the road before reaching the camp. Then I was clattering down the long trail of stone steps, careful not to trip up as I went. I reached the rough track at the bottom and jogged down the track leading to the rifle range where other NCOs stood waiting to mark my score. Falling to the ground I took hold of the magazine they offered. I pushed home the magazine of five .303 bullets into the rifle and lined up my rifle at the target. Breathing heavily from running, I caused the rifle to rise and fall wildly. Sweat trickled from my brow, distorting my vision. But I fired the first shot as soon as I felt calm enough to ease the trigger. It was over. I had had completed the course in a very good time, finishing in ninth place out of twenty-four. It was not world-beating but it made me feel good just the same, knowing how easily I could have stayed with the pack. By making an effort to break free and try to reach the leaders I had helped my cause a good deal. I knew that I would achieve a reasonable mark, hoping to close the gap against poorer efforts in other parts of the cadre.

I wonder now if anyone in the pack resented the effort I had made. Soon after, we were in full battle order with rifles. We were up near the top of the camp mountain, on an exercise in the lush vegetation. I suddenly discovered that my bayonet was not in its scabbard. I searched through the undergrowth but found nothing. At first I thought that someone might have been playing around, having taken the bayonet for a joke. This was a forlorn hope. The truth dawned on me. The bayonet really was missing. I realized the possible consequences of a soldier losing a bayonet and the effects that this would have on my cadre result. Losing a bayonet was not the best way to win officers over. On returning to the barrack room I searched the floor and the area around the building. Nothing. I had no option but to report the loss. In time I was told that I would have to attend an enquiry on the missing article.

An officer interviewed me in an unused barrack room one Saturday morning. He seemed unconvinced after I had told my tale. I had signed for bayonet number 470 and no one had handed in a bayonet with that number. Finally, though, he seemed resigned to accept my story and told me that no penalty would be imposed on my cadre marks. Now it was my turn to be unconvinced. I have wondered since if I had made an enemy in the pack I had left behind during the run. Did someone remove the bayonet from my scabbard, hoping to get me into strife? I was never to solve the mystery but it became more complicated in time. About three months later I signed for a rifle and bayonet one day at Kingston. The bayonet number was 470. There was no point in saying anything by this time and I returned the weapon in the normal way. By that time the cadre was over and my mark known. I had nothing to gain by dredging the matter up.

We were near the end of the course. One hurdle remained: the written exam. This was held in the room usually serving as our dining room, under the supervision of a couple of officers and sergeants. The questions covered the lectures were had been given during the cadre, including questions such as naming the NATO countries and explaining the full title of the organization. I knew that I had done well as the exam ended after an officer stood at my side as I scribbled. He encouraged me with a few exclamations of 'good – good' as I hastened to get down the answers before time ran out. I had a good feeling about the test and hoped to score a high mark, though I was not prepared to come top on the exam. This news, which was leaked to me before the official announcement was great, but it would have to stand against all of the other tests held during the cadre. It was a high note on which to end the course and for a few days after I felt quite light-headed.

With the cadre over I would be returning to Kingston and the MT. After weeks of variety and physical activity I did not find the prospect exciting. Newcastle had things going for it in spite of the poor social life. I would miss the intimate feeling of the smaller camp when back in the big yard of the battalion. I would never again serve at Newcastle after the cadre and look back on it now with affection.

I remember climbing the twisting steps to the small cookhouse that stood on a strip of levelled ground. The cook was short but heavy with fat. He always appeared in a white vest, not always spotless, with a white chef's hat. His arms were wide and flabby, adorned by tattoos. Around his corpulent waist he wore a white cotton apron, splattered in places with food stains. He did not say much but stood behind the table, looking on as our food was dished out to us. This was done by the cook's assistant. He was pleasant and well-liked and who in turn liked the booze and cards a great deal. Also helping out in the cookhouse was a Jamaican called Clint who seemed to be on the official payroll. He was a cheerful, happy-go-lucky man with a wide smile over which sat a well groomed Clark Gable moustache. His colour went well with his physique and he displayed well developed muscles beneath a clean white vest. Clint always had a cheery word as he ladled out the thick, lumpy porridge in the morning or dollops of mashed potato. He was very popular with most people, always interested in what was going on. Clint possessed a great humility, without being servile, and much common sense.

After being given our food along with a mug of sweet tea, we would make our way to the dining-cum-lecture and exam room. This was reached through a tin-roofed walkway. Our fat cook, his assistant and Clint shared quarters that ran along one side of the external wall of the dining hall. Here they flourished in a life that involved no duties except cooking and cleaning up. Booze flowed freely in their quarters and women were known to spend nights there. So long as the food was prepared on time and to a reasonable standard no one seemed to worry. Clint of course was the one who had to get up early to get things started.

I also look back on those cinema nights in the Newcastle church hall, perhaps having scrounged several empty soft drink bottles to find the admission fee. When buying a drink at the NAAFI a small charge for the bottle was included in the price. On returning the bottle the charge would be refunded. When hard up it could be profitable to scout around the camp to search for the price of a cinema ticket or a packet of cigarettes. The cinema cost nine pence and bottles brought three pence. There were lucky times but also times when others had been before and taken every bottle.

There was one night at Newcastle when a group of us went to a dance a little way down the mountain. It was a dance for local Jamaicans but we had been invited, probably by a local passing through the camp. The dance floor was a small courtyard of stone blocks, with kerosene lamps lighting the proceedings: there was no moon. A ramshackle wooden house stood at the side of the court-yard. People danced with sweating faces in the glow of the lamps, dancing to a calypso that stirred the blood. I remember the sensuous rhythm of the dancers and musicians, moving as naturally out of their African past as singing came to Welshmen. Everyone was very friendly to us, even if we were part of an occupying force. They shared food and drink and there were no problems. It was a night of good fun and enjoyment. Many locals arrived as the night progressed and by 10 the place was jumping. Frenzied bodies twisted, writhed and sweated in that confined space. Their hard lives were for the moment forgotten as they gave themselves to the beat of the music, faces wreathed in smiles. This night was memorable for the good time we had mixing and dancing with the ordinary folk of Jamaica. Apart from the few people we would come into contact with in the camps most of our contact occurred only in brothels and clubs. It was good to be among the real people of the island, on a dance floor where they were the masters for a change.

I would come tenth out of twenty-four in the cadre and was more than content with that, competing with men from the rifle companies. Now I felt that my lance-corporal's stripe had been well and truly earned and could hold my own as an infantry NCO. The cadre and its result was for me one of the most satisfying things I had undertaken in Army life to that time.

12

Bayonets to Guiana

Some men of the MT Section welcomed me back as clerk with flattering remarks on having missed my organisational skills but perhaps they thought that their assignments would have been easier with me working out the rosters. I had had a certain skill in dealing with the chess game of MT schedules but now the old zip seemed to have left me. Things developed into a mechanical, day-to-day way of doing things. Going to Newcastle on the cadre had sharpened me up, giving a new perspective on soldiering. Staying in the MT probably meant staying MT clerk, with the regular drivers holding on to their duties as firmly as shit sticking to a blanket, as we said. I was not overly impressed by the prospect. My thoughts of a change of scenery really kicked into gear when I was not minding my own business one afternoon. The day's duties were over for most of the MT except those on essential work. For some reason I was looking around the MT officer's office which was next to the main one. On the desk I found a report on my efforts on the cadre and I did not hesitate to read the comments. One sentence had a great effect on my thoughts of a change of direction: 'he is more intelligent than most men and should be cultivated in a rifle company'. This sentiment finally decided me. I applied for a transfer that was eventually approved. As I had expected, many thought the rocks in my head had been shaken loose. To give up a steady and comfortable number as MT clerk with the power that came with it, to go soldiering in a rifle company did not make much sense to most. Indeed there were some doubts lurking in the shadows of my own mind but I turned away from them to the positive side. At least I would have a great deal more interest in every day living, with more variety too – or so I thought. The transfer came through, placing me with 'D' Company several barrack blocks away, opposite the barrack square. I bade farewell to petrol, oil, trucks and jeeps and headed for a life of pure soldiering with a soldier's best friend – his rifle.

Life in 'D' Company was full of activity during working hours and afterwards. I began playing a lot of sport: mostly soccer and hockey. These games would take place in the afternoon on the huge sports ground at the camp. The battalion ran a 'knockout' hockey competition in which my team did really well for a while before going out. I found I had a natural flair for this game and had some good games along the way to our eventual eclipse. How great it was then, running around like terriers, superbly fit and tanned, playing in the golden glow of the afternoon sun. Then back to barracks for a shower before tea. Lunch was known as 'tiffin' and was usually light with the more substantial meal later after the going down of the sun and heat. The word 'tiffin' went back to the British Army in India, meaning a light, midday meal; luncheon. The menu would be chalked up on a blackboard in the cookhouse.

I became a centre-forward one afternoon, playing soccer for 'D' Company against another company. The opposing team had a couple of really good players including a centre-half who had played for the battalion side. At the end of the day we were thrashed 10-1 but I had the honour of scoring our solitary goal. I remember the scene vividly. The opposing goalkeeper threw the ball to the centre-half who had played in the battalion team, who received it and dribbled his way up field. I raced up to challenge him, getting a tremendous shock when I found I had whisked the ball from his feet. I sped towards the goal with only the keeper to beat but aware of the star centre-half hot on my heels. There would be limited time to steady myself and shoot with him bearing down on me. The ball left my foot with tremendous speed and, from the corner of my eye, I saw the blur of the goalkeeper dive to save the shot. He did save it but only managed to hit the ball away with one hand without full control. I saw the flash of the ball hurtling towards me and, in a reflex action, raised my foot and lifted it high over the goalkeeper's head into the goal. I don't think the noted centre was too pleased with himself but I was thrilled. I felt as if I scored the winning goal in a Wembley cup final. Later I was selected to play for the same team but failed to read the notice board and missed my selection. The game went on without me.

Around this time I became an avid reader, visiting the battalion library on many afternoons. I read eagerly and widely. Among the books I read were George Orwell's *Nineteen Eighty Four* (which seemed a long way off in 1952), *My Early Life* by Winston Churchill and the novel *Moulin Rouge*. I had no knowledge of Toulouse Lautrec before reading this book and became fascinated by his sad but eventful life. A book that made a big impact on me, and on the rest of the world, was the first novel of a young writer called Norman Mailer. I thought it was one of the best war novels of all time, a book of war in the Pacific, *The Naked and the Dead*. I've re-read it since and wasn't as impressed as I had been when I was younger.

Then suddenly routine life came to an end. Trouble had developed in the colony of British Guiana, in South America. A politician named Dr. Cheddi Jagan had been elected Prime Minister. He headed the People's Progressive Party and was regarded by the British government as espousing dangerous communist ideas. The British government, unimpressed with this subversive force (at a time when Britain was fighting communism in Korea) decided to send a military force to depose Jagan and his party. A good part of the battalion was ordered to go to British Guiana to deal with the crisis. A detachment of troops was to fly to Georgetown, Guiana's capital, preceding the main body arriving by sea. I was part of the seaborne contingent. There was a great deal of activity before we found ourselves going by truck along the Palisadoes road one Sunday afternoon to embark for South America. We did not know what to expect but we wrote our wills in our pay books, a sombre indication that we might be expected to fire and be fired on. It was late afternoon in the bright sunshine as we lined up on a ramshackle wooden pier waiting to board the cruiser HMS *Superb*. The *Superb* was part of the Royal Navy's West Indies fleet. Dressed in battleship grey the ship sat in the calm waters of Kingston harbour, waiting for hundreds of pairs of hobnailed boots that were to clatter over a spotless deck. The long line moved slowly but in time I became one of those dragging my kitbag onto the ship.

On going below we found quarters cramped, with members of the ship's crew slinging hammocks for us all over the ship and organising us into messes. Each mess was responsible for looking after itself including meals. A soldier from each mess would collect the food from the ship's galley. I remember huge trays of golden potato chips being delivered to groups of famished squaddies eager to gorge on food of a superior kind than they were used to. Those chips and the tender sausages that accompanied them tasted as good as they looked.

A couple of days out to sea we had an emergency. One of the ship's crew had to be transferred to one of the two accompanying frigates that came alongside in choppy conditions. Many of us lined the *Superb's* rails watching the sailor being winched across the gap of heaving water between the two ships. He sat in a bo'sun's chair attached to a cable which, dipping in the middle, took the man close to the churning sea before rising again as he neared the waiting ship. Eager sailors reached out to pull him in as he swung up at the end of this ordeal. I couldn't help but reflect that this was like something I would otherwise have seen only on the cinema. There seemed an air of unreality about everything that was happening – aboard a cruiser speeding across the Caribbean Sea to who knew what in South America.

Once we listened to a BBC Overseas Service bulletin coming over the ship's tannoy system. Our venture was briefly headline news, telling of the Royal Welch Fusiliers heading south-eastwards to thwart a communist takeover. We were amused at this openness, assuming that it would have been preferable to have kept the operation low key. I am sure that our amusement would soon have evaporated if we had found armed rebels awaiting us in Georgetown.

We learned a little about British Guiana, whose original Arawak and Carib inhabitants had mostly been destroyed in the Spanish conquest. The colony had been captured by the Dutch in the seventeenth century and by Britain during the French Revolutionary War. A mixture of the descendants of Negro slaves and East and West Indians now populated it. About half the population were descended from Indians brought in to work the sugar estates after the abolition of slavery in the 1830s. The colony was self-governing, with local politics dividing along racial lines. The People's Progressive Party (PPP) was Indian-dominated. It was the British government's alarmist reaction to the leftist leanings of the PPP that brought about the present crisis. It was, of course, the Cold War in which western governments looked askance at the idea of even pinkish governments in their former colonies. Britain would have known that it was on safe ground in taking action to deny what it saw as communism gaining a foothold in South America, acting with strong support of the United States. It would be a different story a few years later in 1956 when the Americans gave no support in Britain's ill-conceived incursion to Suez. With the Soviet Union willing to flex its muscles in a Middle East swimming in oil the United States wanted no part of that crisis. In 1953, though, it was regarded as acceptable to send us to British Guiana to maintain democracy by sending the pocket Lenin Dr. Jagan elsewhere. The Fusiliers aboard the *Superb* showed that that the days of sending a gunboat had not quite passed.

Three, perhaps four, days passed before we saw land. We did not go too close, just enough to see a large chunk of land partly hidden in the haze of distance. This, it seemed, was Trinidad so we had reached the shoulder of South America with Georgetown not so far away. Late on a dark night the ships stood off the coast of the British colony watching the lights of Georgetown twinkle in the distance. It was about 2200 hours, with the ship still, as we waited several hours before moving in. I recall leaning on the ship's rail singing 'The Northern Lights of Old Aberdeen' as I watched the cheery lights of Georgetown brighten the darkness. Probably many others and I wondered about our reception on going ashore before turning in for a restless sleep.

Next morning, before dawn, we were in battle order waiting to go ashore and find the answers to our doubts and fears. We were given a hearty hot breakfast before the waiting for something to happen began. This always seemed to be the Army's way. Time dragged on as we watched the darkness slowly merge into bright, tropical daylight. At last something did happen. A civilian ferry boat came close to the *Superb* and we began the transfer on a calm sea. Once in the ferry we sat on hard uncomfortable wooden benches and began another long wait. Now we were much closer to Georgetown and could make out buildings and wharves set out in the style of Belize, I fancied, but on a much larger scale. Everything seemed normal ashore with no sounds of disturbance or gunfire. By now it was bright daylight and we had become so bored with the long wait that we were anxious for something to happen – anything.

The ferry started again moving in slowly towards Georgetown. We approached close enough to see local people spread along the wharf, standing and running along the wooden structure to greet us with looks of fascination rather than anger. We gently touched alongside the wharf as the ferry boat skipper killed the engine, riding the turbulence that swirled about it. The troops began disembarking feeling, I thought, a little self-conscious before the welcoming crowd. Everyone lined up in a relaxed state rather than exhibiting rigid military discipline, sorting out kit bags, pulling up fallen socks, adjusting anklets or doing up undone laces. Some readjusted berets or pulled down belts that had ridden up in the confines of the ferry. One of the Fusiliers' Bren carriers roared to life and began to move off the ferry. Days later I was to discover a photograph in the local press of the carrier coming ashore. It was easy to identify Lance-Corporal Stevens standing on some equipment on the carrier, looking for all the world as if he was directing operations which was certainly not the case. I later bought a large print of the photograph.

What was happening to Dr. Jagan and the people of Guiana beyond the curious crowd on the wharf remained a mystery to us at this stage. Our advance party had flown in earlier so they would have borne the brunt of any reaction. Much later I would learn that Dr. Jagan had made a quick exit from the colony and gone abroad (possibly to India). His forceful American wife, Janet, had fled with him. From all accounts she was an ambitious woman. There had in fact been no armed uprising or anything like one. We heard the story of what had happened to the advance party. They had flown into Georgetown, standing, armed with automatic weapons at the windows of the plane, expecting the worst. They had made for the Governor's residence, protection of the Governor being paramount.

The Royal Welch disembarking at Georgetown, British Guiana, October 1953, with Lance-Corporal Stevens atop the Bren-gun carrier.

The only shot fired was an accidental one. A Royal Welch Fusiliers officer had inadvertently fired his revolver while pulling it out of his holster and had hit a Fusilier in the leg. The wound was not a serious one. So the battalion moved into Georgetown to secure Government House from any potential danger. Many of the local people may have deeply resented our presence but things went no further than this and there was little or no trouble.

We settled in at Georgetown. My memory is a little hazy but I can recall moving into a large hall – near a stables, I think – with a slippery wooden floor. Each man was allocated a space on the floor to place his kit and later given a small mattress to sleep on. Nothing much happened for days after our arrival. I suppose that those in command were aware of the situation but for most of us it came down to trying to make ourselves as comfortable as possible in the circumstances. As disorder and confusion turned into control and understanding we were allowed to go to Georgetown on leave. When we had been allowed out we had little contact with the locals. Georgetown seemed modern enough to my eyes, no backwater on the edge of a jungle. Most things were available including bars and brothels. Life settled into some predictability though we still slept rough with our kit around us. We went to the cinema, in pairs in case of possible trouble. I have a recollection of spending some time on the beach with a local girl but nothing much came of the encounter. I went to see the hit film *Stalag 17*, the prison-camp drama starring William Holden in his Oscar-winning role. He was at the zenith of his career about this time. The film was shown in its original language because most of the population spoke English. I never heard one voice cry out 'British go home' and never saw a gun or a fist raised in anger. In the month I spent in the South American city I found the people to be civil and courteous the whole time.

One day an officer came from battalion headquarters looking for me. He asked me to give him a sample of my handwriting. I did so and after studying my effort he seemed satisfied. I had been doing posters and drawings for various battalion events and assume that I had gained a small reputation. As a result I was offered a position in the battalion's newly-formed intelligence section. I liked the sound of this proposition and accepted, thereby ending my short stint in a rifle company. I was given orders where to proceed and became a founding member of the four-strong section. We moved into a vacant hotel, from where Headquarter Company directed the Fusiliers' operations in British Guiana.

I found myself bed-space behind a reception counter that seemed reasonably comfortable and a better billet than my previous one. It had little space and no privacy and it was likely to be visited by those seeking information at all hours. Once I was awakened by a group of officers – including the commanding officer – wanting to know some information I cannot now recall. I remember jumping up to attention, still in the throes of sleep, trying to give a sensible response in a state of confusion. During the day time the reception area became the intelligence section. Not that there was much information to impart. The maps spread on the reception desk gave a false impression of activity and urgency. With Dr. Jagan having flown the country everything seemed an anti-climax. The show of force seemed to have done the trick. The question was had the British government been unduly alarmist in sending us in or had the Fusiliers' presence tipped the balance in preventing a communist take-over?

Before joining the intelligence section I remember looking out on a tall cricketer practising his batting outside our temporary quarters near the stables. He was of mixed white and coloured ancestry, with the European predominant. His face seemed vaguely familiar in an unsettling way but I was unable to put a name to him. He used the bat with great skill, hitting the ball back to the bowler with firm and sure strokes. The man had class written all over him. Several weeks later, back in Jamaica, I saw the cricketer's face on the sports page of the *Daily Gleaner*. He was the captain of the West Indies team, Jeff Stollmeyer, and there is no doubt that he was the man practising in British Guiana.

In all the battalion spent about a month in the colony before receiving orders to return to Kingston. We were to be replaced by the Argyll and Sutherland Highlanders. At the dockside as we clambered aboard a bauxite boat the band of the Argylls gave us a tremendous send-off, playing a medley of Scottish airs. The swirl of the bagpipes stirred the soul and we felt we were leaving the place in very good hands. The bauxite carrier was to be our home for some twenty-four hours before we met the aircraft carrier HMS *Implacable*. Presumably the aircraft carrier was unable to berth in the shallow water off Georgetown. We found ourselves billets inside the open tanks used for transporting bauxite. Once again the piles of kit surrounding him determined each man's place. In the large metal tanks we were fortunate that the sun was not terribly hot and that it did not rain which would have reduced us to a soggy grey bauxite-stained mess. But the stars formed a bright canopy above us, twinkling through a not-too-uncomfortable night, and soon we rendezvoused with the aircraft carrier.

The *Implacable* had seen service in the Second World War, in the North Sea against the *Tirpitz*, and in the Pacific. Now she was becoming outdated and was used mostly as a training ship for young naval cadets. My first impression of going aboard was how large an aircraft carrier was. When we descended on the lift used to convey aircraft to the deck I was startled to see the huge hangar where we were to be berthed on the voyage to Kingston. It seemed big enough to have held an airship, like being in a huge cavern. Our voices echoed loudly. We were glad to find showers aboard even though the salt-water soap issued refused to lather. We also enjoyed a return to the good food provided by the Royal Navy though it was a notch or two below that served on the aptly-named *Superb*. On the short voyage we did physical training in the mornings on the flat deck of the carrier with the Royal Marine band playing to add spice to the usually boring movements. I remember how good it felt leaping around to the music in the early promise of a new day, looking out across the vast deck on the Caribbean Sea. Old age seemed like a foreign country then, as healthy young men glowed in fitness, sure they would remain so with the immortality of youth.

The young naval cadets, aged fifteen to seventeen, moved around the *Implacable* doing most of the chores and leaving us to enjoy the voyage. Slowly, as the *Implacable* steamed towards Kingston, British Guiana receded in our thoughts. Our month there had been a matter of impending drama without much substance. Needless to say no campaign medal was ever struck for British Guiana, and I have no argument with that but I suppose I could say that I saw active service. The Caribbean was a strong blue, reflecting a lazy pink sky with yellow clouds hanging over the horizon. We looked forward to catching up with the news and all our old haunts. Our Georgetown adventure was about to draw to a close for us as the familiar beauty of Jamaica came into view.

13

Bermuda

So I returned to Kingston as a member of the intelligence section, a part of Headquarter Company. I found myself billeted in a barrack room just a stone's throw from the orderly room – the nerve centre of the battalion. From the orderly room came a steady stream of paperwork: on things about to happen; who was coming and going; promoted or demoted. The intelligence section was to be based at the orderly room in a small side office, away from the busy chatter of typewriters in the main part of the building. On one side of the orderly room was the office of Lieutenant-Colonel Johnson, our Australian-born commanding officer. The orderly room was under the jurisdiction of the battalion's adjutant and the chief clerk with four or five clerks doing the typing, filing and other tasks. These clerks shared the billet into which I moved, a Corporal Jenkins, the latest addition to the intelligence section. The intelligence officer, together with Corporal Jenkins, myself and two lance-corporals from the orderly room made up our staff. We attempted to turn our small office into a comfortable haven but we found ourselves with a lot of time on our hands, with our officer away from us for lengthy periods.

I settled into my new billet, making friends with the orderly room staff, even if one or two of them thought of themselves as coming from a better background than Jenkins and myself. I let the nonsense slide over my head. Because we were all members of the orderly room we were allowed to get away with a lot more than most. There was little in the way of kit inspections, with some of the clerks being excused parades. In many ways we lived a very privileged life.

I began going into Kingston at night, occasionally visiting the fleshpots. For those who had partaken of the sins of the flesh a small building opposite the guardroom was provided to give protection. On collecting a key from the guard-room the building provided facilities to wash the penis before covering it with a cream provided. The cream was also smeared into the urethra. This was supposed to offer some hope in preventing venereal infection. Having to collect a key from the guardroom – where it was obvious what you had been up to – put many men off applying this treatment and they preferred a hot shower instead.

I spent many afternoons in the camp swimming pool. I felt elated on jumping from the diving platform, though not confident enough to dive. I discovered an ability to swim underwater with my eyes open, through a tangle of limbs, enjoying the pool, slithering along the bottom. Without bothering with a towel, I would lie on the flat concrete to dry out in the warm afternoon sun. If funds were good I would saunter over to the pool bar, buying an ice-cold drink or block of chocolate from the ice chest. I would follow things up with a relaxing cigarette before perhaps another bout in the water. With several afternoons of this treatment each week my skin turned as brown as a nut. Even allowing for my smoking, I looked and felt healthy.

One day information circulated through the orderly room that a 'Big Three' conference was to take place on the island of Bermuda. President Dwight Eisenhower, together with Sir Winston Churchill and the French Premier M. Joseph Laniel were to meet on the island to discuss world affairs and, in Ike's case, to play a round or two of golf. This conference brought a welcome break in our routine. The intelligence section would be joining a detachment of the Royal Welch Fusiliers to travel to Bermuda to protect the great men. Members of the band, along with the pioneers and the goat, Billy, would join the party. Before flying to Bermuda we of the intelligence section spent much time enlarging and copying plans of the Ocean View Hotel and its grounds, where the leaders would stay. We enlarged the original maps, making larger-scaled tracings of the hotel and the surrounding area. We then coloured them, using poster paints, colouring the lawns around the buildings green, and so on. I enjoyed making these maps, taking pride in my drawing and painting skills. Everyone involved did an excellent job.

The Saturday morning arrived when we would leave Kingston for Bermuda. We were to board a British Overseas Airways Corporation Stratocruiser at Palisadoes Airport. The Stratocruiser was considered to be 'state of the art' in long distance air travel in 1953. It was powered by four propeller-engines but the days of the jet engine were fast approaching. BOAC were soon to introduce the ill-fated de Havilland Comet. The first of these passenger-carrying jets were found to be fatally flawed after several crashes and many deaths. The Comet was taken out of service and changes made to its structure. By the time it had returned to service, the Americans had taken the lead in jet travel, and they never lost it.

For us, on this bright Saturday, the big aircraft standing on the Palisadoes runway was the latest marvel of the air. We stood awe-struck before being ordered to climb the portable stairway. Before boarding we were photographed

'Billy' the regimental goat of the Royal Welch Fusiliers, as much a member of the regiment as any Fusilier.

The Royal Welch Fusiliers Bermuda contingent (with goat) boarding a BOAC Stratocruiser, with Tom peering uncertainly before his first flight, eighth from left.

for battalion records, standing on the stairs and the runway in company with the battalion goat. The officer, Second Lieutenant William Roach later became famous as the character Ken Barlow in the television series *Coronation Street*. The photograph was later published in the Royal Welch calendar for 1954.

Lieutenant Roach was, I think, a National Service officer. He seemed to be quite popular with the men though I did not know him well – he did not command my platoon. I had been inspected by Lieutenant Roach a few times while mounting guard. The practice was to carry an extra man in the guard and the smartest turned out man would be excused the guard and could march off the parade ground. The chosen man was called the 'stick man'. It seemed to me that the stick man was always a tall man of good physique. Short, skinny men like me did not stand much chance, however well 'bulled up' were his uniform, boots and rifle.

This was the first time I had flown and I must admit to being nervous as the tremendous roar of the Stratocruiser's engines pushed the plane along the narrow runway jutting out to sea. Soon we were high above Jamaica, a small jewel below us in the Caribbean blue as we rose higher into billowing clouds, making our way north toward Bermuda. Looking out of the cabin window I could see the steady turning of the props in a blur of speed reflecting in the bright morning sunshine. I sat in wonderment before noticing the interior of the plane.

I was surprised to see a civilian air hostess, as flight attendants were called then, dressed in a BOAC uniform. As she fussed over our comfort probably a small part of her wished she were elsewhere. For men who did not often encounter beautiful white women it was hard for us not to stare at her every movement as she moved up and down the aisle serving drinks. Another surprise came when we were served a delicious meal on a tray: I tasted asparagus spears for the first time. It was an introduction to a food I have loved ever since. It was novel for us to be waited on like this: a contrast to the rough and ready ways of the battalion cookhouse.

We flew on through the daylight hours, sitting back in our comfortable seats, lulled by the steady drone of the engines. Looking down on the calm sheet of blue water that was the Caribbean, I thought of the sharks probably lurking below and of the horrid possibility of our plane going down. There were enough of us aboard to give the sharks a hearty banquet. I pushed such thoughts down into the cellar of my mind. Looking down we saw large islands made entirely from salt, so we were told – perhaps they were of coral. These islands were as flat as billiard tables, off-white and huge even from our altitude. I wandered what would happen if a human tried to walk on them. I chased these thoughts away, closed my eyes and dozed off for short snoozes, enjoying the flight.

The bright sun which had danced off the water through the day now began to be overtaken by an approaching darkness as we flew over the famed Bermuda Triangle. Once again shadows of fear raced through my mind. This was a time when few people of my background travelled by air. Flying had not then become routine as it has today. Darkness closed around us as we neared Bermuda. We were really returning to the island's capital, Hamilton, because we had called there in the *Dilwara*. The lights of Hamilton sparkled below as we swept down to land on the runway, the Stratocruiser's huge wheels bouncing two or three times as we rolled along. I breathed a sigh of relief, probably along with several others.

Many of us farewelled the pretty air hostess before clambering down to the tarmac. There was a coolness to the night that found its way through our lightweight tropical uniforms. After all, we were now further north and on the edge of the Atlantic. Lining up, we were able to see the crew of the aircraft leaving, exchanging cheerful banter with the hostess as they moved toward the terminal building. I envied their glamorous life. These thoughts ended abruptly as we came to attention to listen to what was expected of us. We climbed aboard the trucks that would take us to a hot meal and a bed.

I was to discover that Bermuda had changed little since my previous visit, in 1951. Hamilton was clean but sterile. It lacked the vitality of Kingston, along with the music of that place in the sun. The locals were friendly but not warm. There were places to go and things to see but the reality was that Bermuda was a playground for the rich and we were on the outer.

The army's headquarters was established under canvas near the Ocean View Hotel. This luxury hotel was situated close to the sea, sitting grandly on grass-covered cliffs. Our large tent buzzed with activity as officers and men prepared for the security of the coming conference. The place was full of maps, on tables and hanging on panels. These included the enlargements we had produced in Kingston. Officers stood around talking in public school accents, leaning on canes, some with generous moustaches being singed by foul-smelling pipes. Everything seemed to be in a general state of confusion but I was heartened to learn that the intelligence section was to remain together as a separate group.

We spent many hours contributing to this confusion with no one certain of what they were supposed to be doing. The map table in the tent bore small flags that meant something to officers who walked about waving their canes and pointing to them with a casual air. Obviously someone must have known what was going on but they were keeping it a close secret. I am sure that a great deal of that time on Bermuda cost the British taxpayer a great deal to no purpose. Of course there was no real threat and the conference passed uneventfully.

One day, walking through the streets of Hamilton, I could hear the stirring sound of a military band. Walking toward the music, I could see a military parade was taking place in the city. Between two buildings I could see Winston Churchill standing on a dais. He stood with a wide smile on his pink, chubby face, taking the salute as the Bermuda Defence Force marched by. He was almost eighty but he looked in fine fettle, very much enjoying the occasion. I thought of the time that Churchill had visited Jamaica – the first time I had seen him in the cherubic flesh. We stood lining the road passing through Up Park camp. As the chauffer-driven car slowly moved through our ranks, with Churchill waving in acknowledgement, we were given the command to cheer. The drill was to raise the right arm to the beret which was then pulled down onto the chest in a set move-ment. Standing with the beret clutched to the breast, an officer called for us to give three cheers in honour of the famous leader. It was a poor effort. Welshmen who had been fed the myth of Churchill sending in Welsh soldiers to shoot Welsh miners early in the century found it hard to give voice. Wales, a stronghold of the Liberal and later Labour Parties, had little time for Conservative politicians, even Churchill. A weak series of hip-hip-hoorays rose from the men who looked almost embarrassed as Churchill's car passed. I felt a little self-conscious. Winston beamed as though entering Rome after a magnificent victory, a fixed smile on his face. I felt for the man, a very strained reception – almost squirming as the car moved away down the line, with the hoorays not getting any louder or more enthusiastic. But if he was many things, Churchill was also a politician, with the hide of one, and he took it in his stride. I did admire Winston Churchill for his great service during the Second World War.

While on Bermuda I heard the stories of Churchill's fondness for the whiskey bottle. Tales told of Churchill getting into the hotel lift, unsteady on his feet and belligerent with drink, circulated among the troops protecting the conference. I myself never saw this side of the man. These stories emanated from the members of the Royal Welch on guard duty around the hotel. Perhaps they should have paid more attention to that task. I heard how a member of the American secret service, protecting his president, decided to test how effective the military pres-ence actually was. He managed to worm his way into the hotel without having to use the password to get through the guard – and there was hell to pay.

Our cookhouse was also set up under canvas near the hotel. There we mixed with members of the Royal Marine detachment, the American secret service and the Bermuda Defence Force. With this force the three world leaders had good protection. I never caught a glimpse of 'Ike' or the French leader. I seem to remember there being a rambling golf course on the cliffs on which the Ocean View Hotel sat. I am sure that Eisenhower found his way there during the conference.

Whatever world-shaping decisions were arrived at during these three-power talks, the time came to pack up and return to Kingston. After a couple of weeks I felt glad enough to return, the Bermuda adventure having paled a little with the general boredom of the event. There after-hours entertainment offered little to off-duty soldiers. After several hours of relaxation aboard the Stratocruiser, stretched out in comfortable seats and another fine meal, we were circling over Kingston. Coming down to land at Palisadoes, it felt almost as if we were coming home.

I resumed soldiering in Kingston, returning to the orderly room staff's barrack room. The intelligence section re-grouped in our old room but the lack of stimulation continued. Our mornings usually involved appearing to be active which can be more tiring than actually being busy. The sun-drenched afternoons offered time on the mattress reading for hours, or a dip in the pool or sport. It was usually foolish to go to sleep and sleep through the daytime heat. Waking up felt lousy, and left you feeling like a stunned mullet, an effect that continued until bedtime, when it was then impossible to sleep. Then it would be a business of thrashing about under the mosquito net until in the early hours sleep finally came. It was better somehow to get through the afternoons one way or another and drop off to sleep easily and naturally after talking in the dark after lights out.

Lying there in the dark, body and mind in pleasant anticipation of a night in repose, and sleep which could transfer you out of the army in dreams, if only until the bugle cut through the new day. Men having their last cigarette of the day drew smoke into their lungs, the red glow bright enough to illuminate their features. A man might stumble into the room, trying to find his bed through a mist of drink. The daring ones would flick on the light, to the annoyance of those trying to sleep, attempting to undress hastily before the light was extinguished.

It was good when the light went off, hiding the room and its usual mess. The table covered in empty soft drink or beer bottles and an ashtray, often improvised from the lid of shoe polish tin, full of butts and ash. There might be a greasy candle stuck in its own grease in another tin lid where earlier in the evening someone had held their boots or civilian shoes over the naked flame. With plenty of saliva spat on the footwear and a spot of polish rubbed in with a rag in small circles over the leather the boots or shoes would glow. A copy of the *Daily Gleaner* usually showing the sports page upwards could be on the wooden table. Mugs with cold tea would stand there, brought from the NAAFI hours before. A banana skin might be there or a pack of well-used playing cards: one or two fallen the floor. Come the morning all hands will rally to the cause to get the barrack room fit for a possible inspection.

But in the still tropical night it was good to snuggle up for sleep – the mess could look after itself until morning. A rasping drawn out fart might come from somewhere in the room: everyone hoping it will be a dud with no suffocating aroma seeping its way to reluctant nostrils. By now perhaps the soldier who had come in the worse for drink might be out in the toilet block vomiting, not all of which will find its way into the toilet bowl. It will stay splashed around the floor, waiting in ambush for anyone silly enough to go for a pee in bare feet and in the dark later in the night.

A favourite game played in barrack rooms was that of making a French bed. Most men would make up their beds at the close of the day's duties. Sometimes a man going out would return to a bed that had been re-made in his absence by his companions. This time, however, the top sheet would be folded in such a way as to allow him to get his feet only half way down. Soldiers coming in late in the dark and perhaps tiddly could have men trying to fathom why their feet would reach down only so far as they kicked the sheets furiously. Of course no one ever owned up to being the culprit. Still, living in the billet with the headquarter company clerks was a bit more civilized than life in a rifle company or with the MT.

Towards the end of 1953 life for one of the men in this barrack room would change dramatically.

14

Marcia

One Sunday evening a group of us had gone off to see a film at the Carib Cinema. Coming out to an evening that still had some life to it we decided to call at the Silver Slipper for a couple of cold beers. It was a warm evening and we sat enjoying our Red Stripes.

This evening there seemed to be more activity than was usual at the Slipper. From above us came the sound of dancing and music told us that the jukebox was well fed. Curious, we carried our beers up the wooden stairway to the spacious dance floor. Three or four Jamaican women danced in time to the catchy tunes, unusually not calypso but modern dance music. I found this in itself intriguing. Two girls, I fancy, danced together. We sat around a metal table, enjoying a cool breeze on the verandah. I leaned back on my chair watching the women on the dance floor as I sipped my beer and smoked a cigarette. The one who had an instant attraction for me was certainly no mere girl. She appeared to be well into her twenties, with a pale white skin but obviously with coloured blood, told by the nostrils that were part of an attractive, if not beautiful, face. The woman was not large in the bust but her tight clinging dress showed up her rounded bottom that moved sensuously as she danced.

I decided to ask her for a dance, moving quickly as the record changed. Surprisingly she said yes, sliding easily into my arms, melting into my body, soft and yielding. I did not speak for some time, savouring her closeness, dancing to a sentimental fox trot, which I had not done for a while. Before the dance ended I made some small talk, to which she responded warmly and naturally. I walked back to my table feeling as though the sun had just come out on my heart: eager to have another opportunity to hold her in my arms. I approached her again eventually. She agreed to another dance with genuine warmth. Her name was Marcia, I was able to discover as we whirled around the room, eyed by my companions at the table. I felt good to see them looking with some envy at the woman I held close, putting some extra zest into my dance steps as we passed them. We danced again and again as the evening sped by. I found out that Marcia and her friends were on their way to a party and had called into the Slipper on the way. It had been a whim to stop there Marcia told me. Before she prepared to leave with her friends I attempted to make arrangements to see her again. She would not give a firm commitment but because of her manner I did not feel discouraged. A charge of sexual energy passed between us and I was completely captivated. When she left the Slipper I bade farewell to my mates, following Marcia and her group to the bus stop for central Kingston. This bus would pass Up Park camp but that seemed incidental as I climbed aboard behind the women. The bus was full but I managed to work my way through the passengers standing in the aisle until I was able to speak to Marcia, asking if it would be possible to go to the party with her and her companions. By now the bus had passed the camp so I had burned my boats anyway.

Marcia agreed to let me go with them to the party and we got off the bus not far beyond the camp. My memory of the party was and still is a very vague one. I had drunk a few beers at the Slipper and continued drinking at the party. I am able to recall sitting talking to Marcia outside later in the evening somewhere not far from the sea. I could hear the gentle lapping of the waves. I attempted to get romantic. Marcia was firm in her refusal but she was prepared to meet me the next evening. We arranged to meet at the Spot, near Up Park camp outside Uncle's before going to see a film at the Carib. Eventually I left to begin the trek back to camp with no buses running that late. I made a short cut or two on the journey, a journey on which I ran through the evening in my thoughts. In what seemed like no time at all – it was somewhere around 2 a.m. – I was strolling by the two big cannons on either side of the camp gates. After booking in at the Guard Room I headed for my bed and a few hours of sleep, still enjoying the remembrance of the night that had passed. It was a long time before I fell asleep.

Next evening the time finally arrived for me to walk to the Spot to meet Marcia. She had been in my thoughts through most of the working day. As I neared Uncle's I could recognise Marcia standing in the shadows. My pulse quickened with the realisation that she had turned up. It was dark and the neon lights of the Spot were flashing, shedding enough light to see comfortably. The odd bus and car sped by as we began the short walk to the Carib. Many locals walked the streets of this small city within a city. The Spot was very popular with the troops as it featured within its bounds most, if not all, of what a soldier expected. As well as the Silver Slipper and the Carib, which was a very fine cinema indeed, there was an open-air cinema about half a mile down the road.

On the walk to the cinema with Marcia I felt almost embarrassed now that I was free of alcohol. I made small talk as we passed the Spot bookshop that fascinated me so much. I often browsed among the stands of paperbacks: expensive

A street in Kingston, the scene of much of Tom's off-duty life in Jamaica.

even then on a soldier's pay. But I was not going in there this night, walking along with this attractive woman, attempting to recover some of the alcohol-induced debonair spirit of the evening before. Coming at last to the illuminated entrance to the picture house, several people joined us as we climbed the steps to the foyer. I had a view of Marcia's face: well made-up – in the glare of the brash lighting, her pale white skin, actually paler than my own sun-bronzed face. And yet she could not pass as a European; appearing as a coloured woman who had been bleached white: the broad nose, the short, wire-like hair. She had also the generous lips of the black African. Painted with red lipstick, her lips wrapped up a heart-wrenching smile. All in all, this woman was for me most desirable.

Used by now to brothel-creeping, it was a strange experience to be sitting in the darkness of a cinema on a date with a woman. I can't recall the name of the film but think I would have enjoyed it even if it had been on my list of the ten worst movies ever made. Looking quickly at Marcia, intent on the screen, I could hardly believe my fortune in having gone to the 'Silver Slipper' on a random night to meet this attractive, mature and warm person. After the film we caught the bus at the same spot where we had left for the party the night before. Marcia motioned to me when to stand to leave the bus, once again a short distance past the camp. Leaving the main road we walked along side roads and once down and then up a stony, grassy gully. After a time we moved through a tree and bush-covered piece of ground. Here I attempted to be amorous but Marcia whispered 'Not here'. She guided me a short distance further, to a clearing near a collection of wooden buildings, one of which was Marcia's shack.

It was small, with the bed filling up most of the bedroom. There were a couple of pieces of bedroom furniture but it was very humble. There was only one other room, a sort of combined living and eating room with a table and some chairs in one corner. It was not by any means grand but it was adequate for survival, and clean.

Marcia and I undressed quickly and went to bed. I found her sexually very exciting, very knowledgeable in the art of love. Although I had had some sexual experience Marcia extended my learning a great deal. She taught me positions and techniques that became the foundation of a lifetime of sexual fulfillment. It was obvious that she was well versed in sexual experience and I responded to her ardour with all the vigour of a youth not long past twenty. Afterwards I lit up a cigarette and relaxed on the bed, naked on the sheets, the only mattress covering. We got onto the subject of age and Marcia gave hers as twenty-nine. She lay alongside me, naked too, and I studied her shapely figure; with her breasts now drooping and on the smallish side. On her buttocks she had taut, firm flesh, and her hips too had resisted going to fat. Coming to the end of the cigarette, I thought about returning to camp.

Marcia explained the route of a short-cut that would bring me out near the camp at the sports field entrance. By the time I was signing in at the Guard Room it was into the early hours but I was pleased with myself for having followed Marcia's directions. In time went I was to get to know this trek like an old friend. One morning at about two I amazed a young Jamaican man as we stopped to chat. He wondered whether I was wise to be about so late, walking alone. It was obvious that being white and a soldier made me far more vulnerable than he was but in the flush of my affair with Marcia and the invincibility of youth I had not thought much of it. I did not stop the practice but became more wary of the possible risks. Still, while walking in the early hours I hardly saw anyone and not once did I have problems.

I now met Marcia regularly. Going to her shack became the mainstay of my existence. Slowly details of Marcia's life emerged during conversations after sex. Her husband had left her, leaving her with two small children to support and there were no social services to call on. Gradually the full picture would emerge.

There were times when Marcia put on the mantle of another life. She would be picked up by a car, taken to a party or function and expected to provide sexual favours for a fee divided between her and the organisers. Or so I presume: I was never told the full details but came to understand that this part of Marcia's life was completely separate to her other life. I had to accept Marcia on this level or I would cease to be a part of her life. It was made clear to me, mostly without the use of words, that Marcia's 'holidays' were ironclad in their necessity. Nothing could stand in the way, even her feelings for me. It was not easy for me to accept this situation. She seemed to be two people with two lives. One part of her was the kind, generous, loving Marcia, as she was to me, telling me of her strict child-hood, brought up by a family with sound values.

The hours I spent with Marcia were mostly free of argument – apart from my harping on her double life – and hours of passion that bonded us with a kind of love. For me – at the age I was – it probably came down to a basic need for sex. Marcia offered it freely and mostly when I wanted it. I never paid Marcia for sex though when we went out everything was on me, as was the custom. Even so, I became close to the woman simply for herself, her nature and personality. The relationship could end and I would be back to the alternatives of going to brothels or staying celibate. I chose to stay with Marcia, accepting her 'holidays' as the price of the good times I had with her. We were both aware that our relationship was never going to lead anywhere and was little but a rest haven off the main road of our lives. I shut out Marcia's other life: locked it away in the dungeon of my mind. It was easier that way. For Marcia, of course, I suspect that I was the other life where she had some kind of normality, some way to allow her emotions come to the surface, to love and hopefully to be loved – or at least to be thought of as a human being and not as a commodity to be purchased. Although the sex was an important part of our life together I felt a great fondness for Marcia, even if it was not love. We enjoyed each other's company, each fulfilling a need in the other.

After my working day as a soldier I left camp every evening it was possible, going to Marcia's home as a married man returning to his beloved at the end of the day. We both knew there was no future for us together, taking what we had, savouring it for the moment, as each moment would eventually become the past, to remember in old age, as I do now. As I write this Marcia, if she still lives, will be over eighty. I wonder now if I am in a corner of her memories, memories of a time long ago when I was young and mostly stupid and as she was mature and serene. She was caught in a whirlpool in which she could stay afloat only as long as she remained young and attractive. What would be her fate when the shadows crept over her? By now that fate will have been decided and I can only hope that fortune has been kind to her: perhaps in a good marriage or some other happiness.

We had many good times. We would go to the cinema, as any courting couple would do, going for a creamy milkshake afterwards to talk about the film. I suspect a neighbour looked after her children. I remember going with Marcia to see Doris Day and a young Danny Thomas in *I'll See You in My Dreams*, a musical romance based on the life of the songwriter Sammy Kahn. It was a typical sugar and syrup love story of the 'fifties. It was a time when many people still had not become cynical and violence mostly happened only on the screen. There was plenty of violence going on in a place far away called Korea of course. But at home people were able to walk down a darkened street, even women. Drugs were kept at the chemist's, in hospitals or doctors' surgeries. We all lived in a kind of naïve innocence, watching films of utter hokum! Doris Day appeared virginal and correct with song-writer Danny managing to write hit songs with a minimum of effort. Sitting in the packed cinema with Marcia, watching this romantic feast in the darkness, I recall that it seemed to bring us closer that night and make us forget the reality of our situation. Every once in a while *I'll See You In My Dreams* turns up on television. Although I haven't watched it for nearly fifty years even seeing it advertised makes me recall that night in Kingston.

Once Marcia and I went to a dance place by the sea. It was on the same lines as The Glass Slipper where we had met: a large wooden dance floor, some tables and chairs. The water could be seen through the open verandah on one side of the spacious, shiny floor. Everything was on one level. It was late in the afternoon as we sat having a drink or two. We were the only people there apart from the Jamaican barman and a waiter or two. The sea came up to the edge of the dance floor, below the wooden wharf on which the building stood. The sea breeze gently played around where Marcia and I sat. A number of sea gulls dive-bombed outside, squawking furiously among themselves. The golden sun was low in the sky, moving slowly toward the calm horizon. Marcia and I spent a pleasant time, dancing to a record around the deserted floor, with all the space we could want, trying some fancy steps. This is a scene I retain in my memory album.

Life was going along at an enjoyable pace. My work with the intelligence section was certainly not strenuous, with my time after work mostly spent with Marcia. But one night things changed dramatically when I fell asleep at Marcia's place after we had made love. I slept deeply through the night with Marcia at my side. The night was rolling back to the brightness of a Jamaican day when I awoke suddenly. It was a week-day so I had to sign on at the camp by 0600 hours.

One glance at the time told me instantly that I could not possibly make it. Even if I ran all the way (which was impossible) I could not arrive before 0610. I knew that I was in trouble and decided to return at a brisk pace. Marcia was awake by this time and she listened as I explained the position. I told her that I might not be seeing her for some time. I headed off into the Kingston morning with the sun still struggling to get up, a couple of locals staring as I appeared so early in the day. The day was going to be hot, with the air already humid. I found myself hurrying, the sweat at my armpits soaking through my shirt. Back at the camp the bugler was playing reveille.

I fooled myself as I walked, hoping for a miracle. Perhaps I might be let off with a caution, told to move off to my barrack room and be more careful in future. Cold reality hit me smack in the sweating face as I climbed the few steps to the Guard Room, to see Provost Sergeant Ianto Evans on duty. He had the reputation of being a very tough customer, short but wide and bulky, with a broken nose on a well-worn face. I was to discover eventually that the man was a stickler for the book – the Army's book, that is. While he was able to get down in the pit and bruise with the best, he was fair and just to everyone in applying the rules. The sergeant was surprisingly civil but still recorded my late arrival, which in the end was a matter of twenty minutes. By Army regulations I had already been reduced to the rank of Fusilier – that was automatic even before I appeared on Commanding Officer's Orders to face the charge of being absent from camp at reveille. I left the Guard Room for my barracks and a shower.

I was told to put on my best gear and appear before Lieutenant-Colonel Johnson, who commanded the Royal Welch. By common battalion folklore he was supposed to have been born in Australia. He was extremely short and wore a ginger-brown moustache, the typical army officer growth. I stood on the verandah outside the CO's office, waiting my turn to appear before him, trying to put a story together that I could use in my defence. I was suddenly brought to attention by the Regimental Sergeant Major, and then marched in at quick time to the CO.

Colonel Johnson was sitting at his desk looking over my charge sheet in front of him,. I crashed to attention before him, my eyes fixed ahead. After the RSM had stated my crime, a silence followed during which I was still thinking furiously. At last I was getting a story together which would sound better than the truth even if it would not save my hide completely. When he asked what I had to say in my defence I launched into a tale of fantasy with only a few threads of truth holding it together. As I spun the yarn I amazed myself with my unaccustomed audacity. I told of a farewell party I was supposed to have attended. This imaginary party had occurred at the Half Way Tree, which usually drew a better class of Jamaican, in honour of a young woman about to leave to study in, of all places, Cambridge. I told how I had drunk rum at the farewell and, not being used to it, had passed out, sleeping through until dawn. I had, so the story continued, made a super-human effort to reach camp before 0600 but had failed by some minutes. There were echoes of Cinderella rushing home from the ball, with a grain or two of the young lady going to Cambridge even if the timescale did not fit. This part of the tale was of course based on Lisetta de Barovier's departure some time before. Claiming to be ill-used to rum was particularly cheeky in the light of my escapade In Newcastle in 1951 when I had spent a week confined to the small guard room because of the effects of Jamaican rum. If this adventure still stood on my record – and there was every chance that it did – then I was exposing myself to danger in that Colonel Johnson could say that I had not learnt much over time. Among the stories circulating through the barrack rooms one was that crime sheets were wiped clean after a period, serious crime excepted. This could have been true – I still have no idea – but I took the gamble on my 1951 transgression being overlooked and it seemed to pay off. My relationship with Marcia must have been common knowledge in the orderly room so I wonder if Colonel Johnson generously let me off.

The CO did not begin to chide me on my drinking woes or lecture me on people who never learned. Instead he sat looking down at the paperwork, saying nothing for some time. When he did speak it was a fairly mild warning on the dangers of young men drinking more than they could handle, a homily to which I repeatedly nodded in all the right places. And then – to my astonishment – the CO dismissed the charge without further ado. I shall never know if he knew I was spinning a yarn, rewarding me for my cheek, or if he actually swallowed the whole thing. When I left the army my discharge book read 'Conduct: exemplary' so I must have got away with it. Now I must admit I don't feel proud of myself at this deception but at the time it seemed to be the only thing to do. My relationship with Marcia must have been common knowledge in the orderly room so I wonder if he knew everything and generously let me off.

I marched back out onto the verandah a free man. I knew, of course, that the dismissal of the charge did not mean that I was getting out of it unscathed. The loss of my stripe could not be reversed within several weeks. I would now have the task of removing the stripe from my shirts and jacket. This would leave an outline on the material where the stripe had been and advertise to everyone my fall in rank. But I was elated that I had escaped 'jankers'. If I had received several days of jankers I would not have been allowed to leave the camp. The punishment's proper name was CB ('confined to barracks') but there was a sting in the tail. Apart from not being allowed to leave camp there were the delights of having to report for fatigue duties after the day's work. Nor did the joys end there. It was possible to spend an entire evening racing to and from the Guard Room attired in various states of dress, from best dress down to PT outfit of vest and shorts. The unfortunates on jankers would collapse into their beds for a brief break from their miseries at the end of a long day.

So I had done well, all things considered, and I was still free to leave the barracks in the evenings to see Marcia, and that very evening I was off again to tell Marcia the good news. She was very sorry about the loss of the stripe but glad that I had not lost the privilege of being able to sleep out. I made sure that I did not again fall asleep at her place again, leaving at a reasonable hour to get a good night's sleep in barracks.

There was a postscript to this incident which showed how relations stood between officers and men. About a week later I dressed in civilian clothes to leave camp to see Marcia. I entered the Guard Room to sign out for the evening and in doing so ran into the Provost Sergeant Ianto Evans. As I was signing my name the orderly officer called me aside and asked me what I was doing in civilian clothes in view of my recent charge. I explained that the charge had been dismissed and I was still entitled to wear civilian clothes. He became very aggressive, telling me that I was wrong and that I should return to my barrack room to change into uniform before I could leave camp. I had no option but to comply. I walked to my room very angry. By my understanding of my case there had been no conviction or penalty. The stripe had gone but that was automatic. Why was this officer an officer if he could not understand this, I wondered? But if I wanted to see Marcia there was little I could do but change into my uniform pronto.

While doing so I was surprised to see the orderly officer pass the window of my room. He entered, swishing the air with his cane, informing me that Sergeant Ianto Evans had advised him that I should be allowed to wear civilian clothes if I wished. Of course the Provost Sergeant, being a stickler for the book, had agreed with my interpretation of the rules and he had told the officer that he was wrong. Sergeant Evans quite properly had not corrected the officer in my presence. The officer did not offer any sort of apology, simply leaving the room leaving me feeling that I had got the better of him. Dressed in civvies again I set off for Marcia's.

I had built up a lot of leave during my stay in the West Indies. I had intended to keep most of it for my return to Britain but I decided to surrender seven days to spend with Marcia. This would still leave me several weeks when I did return to Britain. Marcia was enthusiastic so I put in my application. When it was granted I piled some clothes and a razor into a suitcase and set off, a little self-consciously, for Marcia's place.

The first few days we spent together went well. We lived as husband and wife, making love and enjoying our meals together. There was a cold-water shower in the yard, open to the elements through a flimsy wooden lattice-work door. Once Marcia in a playful mood came into the yard as I showered, turning the water on and off between the laughter. It was about the third or fourth day of my leave when Marcia suggested that I should return to camp. I was confused and she was very jumpy. But when I looked out of the tiny window of the bedroom and spotted the car discreetly parked up the lane I understood. A man – a fat, squat Jamaican – sat behind the wheel patiently waiting for someone, I guessed Marcia. There was an 'assignment' for her to escort. Marcia explained how this just happened to come up and it was better if I called off what remained of my leave and returned to Up Park camp. I felt as if someone was twisting a hot poker into my gut, with a lost empty feeling overwhelming my thoughts. We had a brief discussion but Marcia was very forceful and determined, giving the impression that she had little choice in the matter. I reluctantly shoved my things into the suitcase while the man in the car waited – hardly moving, spy-like in the gentle shadows of the lane. A variety of emotions raced through my mind as I made my way back, with the suitcase making me feel more ridiculous than when I had travelled in the opposite direction. It was as if I thought everyone would see me and know that I had been kicked out. This was not the truth, of course, but youth has a habit of magnifying all things, pleasant and otherwise.

I spent the remainder of my leave moping around the camp. I simply read until it was time to go back to work in the intelligence section. I could not help but dwell on Marcia's 'assignments' making myself very miserable. For a week or so I kept out of the picture before eventually giving in to the desire to see Marcia once more. When I arrived at her place she was so pleased to see me and was her usual loving, attentive self. She steered the conversation away when I tried to talk about her other life, as she always did, as if it was a twin sister who lived the life of a Kingston prostitute. In the end I learned to accept that which had to be accepted. We resumed our full relationship with Marcia showing me the many ways to express love in ways I had not known before and for a little while longer we were happy.

15

Our last days

Soon my lance-corporal's stripe was restored, giving me back the task of taking my shirts to the battalion tailor to be re-striped. One or two of my shirts had survived – I had rolled my sleeve up to cover the rank during my brief disgrace.

I did not see a lot of Marcia's children. They came and went and I never really did know who looked after them most of the time. We had a meal at Marcia's once with the children at the table and I attempted to be pleasant and interested but I doubt if I made much of an impression. I was very young, very selfish and with limited horizons. Marcia was the sun in my life and I was not that interested in her satellites. I must be honest – I never really tried to be the friendly 'uncle' to either of them. I do feel more than a little sad about this, with echoes there of my own childhood during the war when my own mother brought a soldier home.

Then Marcia became pregnant. It could certainly be said 'but who is the father?' but Marcia was adamant it was mine. I talked romantically about sending money out from Britain in support but as usual Marcia was more practical. She decided to have an abortion – a 'back street' one of course. Nothing could be said to change her mind. It would cost but Marcia said that she had enough funds to take care of it. One night on my usual visit she said that it had happened, with everything under control. She was very distressed though about the man who had carried it out. He had offered to do the abortion free if Marcia consented to have sex with him first. Marcia had refused the offer, suffered pain and humiliation, paid the creep and left. I understood her anguish as anger swelled in me. There are many dark shadows in the gutter: the abortionist was one of them.

Our relationship was sometimes turbulent. One time Marcia and I had a falling out over something that has long since been forgotten but it seemed serious enough at the time to make me stop visiting. I missed her deep down inside even if I told myself that the whole business had ended. Then a package arrived in the mail. Marcia had sent me a colourful tie as a peace offering, which was enough to undo all my resolve. I was off to see her that very night and things slipped back to the routine of the way things had been between us.

Another time we fell out over a trivial thing that turned out to be more serious. We did not see or contact each other for weeks. I must confess that I had not wiped her from my thoughts as, like an old song, she kept coming back in them. I went off one night with a few lads of the orderly room to have a look at a night club that was ten minutes from Marcia's house. We drank and smoked, telling jokes as soldiers do, watching the locals dance to the band. Perhaps it was the alcohol but as I began thinking of Marcia, an intense longing welling up in me. Suddenly I knew that I was going to go and see her. I told the others where I was going and one volunteered to accompany me on the walk up the steep hill to Marcia's place. We hardly saw anyone as we walked, perhaps a little affected by drink, through the built up area which led to open ground at the top, with a rough lane leading to Marcia's. It was darker walking down the lane but we were able to negotiate the stones and undergrowth without too much trouble. There was the welcome sight of a strip of light under Marcia's door, so it seemed that she was at home. I had thought of the possibility of her not being there. I knocked, excitement flowing with the alcohol in my veins. Marcia came to the door and I could see the pleasure in her eyes when she saw who stood there. In no time at all we were the best of friends again and she accepted the invitation to accompany us back to the club. My mate and I sat waiting in the little house as she dressed and made up. She looked stunning to me. I reflect now on the quality Marcia had of not holding grudges. She was not a doormat but had a special softness that was hard to resist. Once we had made up, everything stayed in the past and there was no back-biting afterwards: a rare quality in women.

The three of us set off down the hill to join the others. I could see that my companion was impressed with Marcia's beauty and her other qualities, which gave me a small glow of pride. I anticipated introducing her to my mates. Everyone was taken by her appearance and gentle, unassuming charm and we spent a couple of hours in good-hearted banter sprinkled with plenty of drink. I also took Marcia out onto the packed dance floor, enjoying being with her again while dancing to some sentimental music. A wonderful evening ended with the others returning to camp while I took Marcia home. We cemented our reunion in bed. It was the early hours of the morning before I reached the camp, falling thankfully into bed for too few hours sleep before rising with bloodshot eyes to face another military day. Once again Marcia and I were together and I felt good inside.

It was approaching Christmas 1953. It would be my last Christmas and last full year in Jamaica. The battalion was earmarked to return to Britain in the coming March, which meant only a matter of three months to run. The orderly room staff decided to put on a Christmas party for themselves and we obtained permission to use the lecture room. We set about decorating the walls in the spirit of the season, with my contribution a poster wishing everyone a 'Merry Xmas 1953'. We had balloons around the room and a huge Union Jack draped down one wall. I felt it may have been intended as a celebration of something beyond Christmas: perhaps it was raising the curtain on our last days on the island.

As some of the men had met Marcia I suggested that she come to our gathering which everyone seemed happy enough to agree to. Marcia in turn was pleased to be asked. When the night arrived I walked about halfway to Marcia's place, where I had arranged to meet her. She looked radiant, a picture to behold in the light dress she had chosen to wear. We slowly walked and talked our way up the long straight road after entering the camp, past the playing fields where, earlier in the year the battalion had organized a tattoo to celebrate the young Queen's coronation. Now the vast space was empty and still as Marcia and I wandered through the warm evening. The small grandstand that had been packed with spectators watching the battalion band, the pioneers and the goat marching and playing in the glare of lights now stood stark and peaceful. At our little party there was plenty of cold beer to drink, kept that way in a chest of chipped ice. Everyone had made some financial contribution, with long white-clothed tables groaning

The Royal Welch's goat mascot, 'Billy', leading the white-aproned Pioneers in the Queen's birthday parade in Kingston, June 1953. Tom is somewhere in the column of troops behind the Pioneers.

with goodies. I sat with Marcia, as a king with his queen. Feeling certain I was envied by most of the men there. Marcia easily handled being the only woman present, and really seemed to enjoy the singing of Welsh airs, which would have been a new experience for her. With the beer flowing we had hearty renditions of all the Fusiliers' repertoire of drinking songs, such as 'Guide me Oh Thou Great Jehovah' and the tear-jerking 'We'll Keep a Welcome in the Hillsides'. I enjoyed the attention shown to Marcia but she stayed at my side the whole evening. It was a happy memory in the making. Later Marcia and I re-traced our steps to her house, sealing the end of a memorable night.

Around this time I went with Marcia to the night club near her home. We had a romantic evening dancing and sitting at our small table, where a wandering photographer took our picture. Later this photograph went with me to Britain along with a studio photograph of her. I destroyed them, along with other images of previous lovers, when I married. Now all these years on it is difficult to form an image of Marcia in my mind though strangely, I remember the spotted dress she wore in the studio photograph. As usual we enjoyed dancing, whirling around in a room packed with Jamaicans. As a European I stood out in this place this particular night but there was another white man there, one I recognized as an officer from the battalion. He seemed most interested in Marcia and I as we danced by, as if he knew me from somewhere but was unable to put me in focus in his brain. I don't know if he did work out eventually who I was but I made the deliberate point of dancing close to his table, giving an exhibition of some fancy footwork as I passed.

Marcia and I would lie in the darkness on her bed, talking on many topics. I would sometimes sing to her – songs such as 'We'll gather Lilacs' which she liked very much. I was a Welshman, slightly homesick, singing of walking down an English lane in a song written by another Welshman, Ivor Novello. As I sang of returning to my homeland, for Marcia it would be a song of farewell. But she always wanted whatever I wanted and was glad for me. We talked of her childhood in Jamaica and of her married life before her husband departed the scene. She was still reluctant to talk of her other life and she would say little of it, except that it was both necessary and distasteful to her. Even in those pre-AIDS times there were risks, of course. The chance of pregnancy she had already encountered. Then there were the risks of VD, especially syphilis. I too was dicing with fate: all the Fusiliers who slept with Jamaican women threw the dice every time they did so. One or two men had understandings with certain women in brothels, borrowing funds from the madam regularly as a side-benefit to the sexual relationship. Youth always believes that misfortune happens to others and I was no exception. Marcia was certainly sexually appealing, but we both found we met in each other needs that suited the two of us. For me she was a life outside the army: for her I probably compensated for her sordid other life. So the relationship continued in spite of the pressures, in spite of the risks. I had wild thoughts that drifted through my head at the time, and even later, after I had returned to Britain. I thought of returning to the island when I had left the army in 1954. They were never practical thoughts, only romantic day dreams, probably put into my head after seeing too many Hollywood films.

Now, these many years later, I would certainly wish to return to the West Indies and Jamaica in particular. I would like to know what became of Marcia and her two children. Perhaps she died long ago. If not, she is over eighty as I write and I can only hope that her journey has not been hard. It would be moving to walk the streets of a now independent Jamaica, to see how some things have changed and how others have stayed the same. One thing I am sure of – the sun still sparkles above a very blue Caribbean. Once perhaps I could have dreamt about going back, to gaze again at Kingston from the Blue Mountains, or perhaps walk again among the graves at Newcastle of soldiers a long time gone. But I know now that these things can never happen.

With Christmas of 1953 over Marcia and I arranged to spend New Year's Eve at the Glass Bucket night club. The incoming year of 1954 would be a turning point for me, apart from returning to Britain. Around the first week of September I would complete my five years with the colours, leaving the army to go into the reserve for the next seven years. I flirted with the idea of signing up again as a regular but I did not take it seriously. Deep down in my shoes I knew it would not happen. Although in many ways the army was a good life I was looking forward to being in control of my life again, making my own decisions once more.

So Marcia and I went out to celebrate this significant year, a year that would also see us parting. As usual Marcia looked wonderful, which made me feel good in spotting Bert Yale sitting at a table with Marietta de Barovier, out to celebrate also. It always gave me a flush of pleasure to be out with Marcia, and this night was no exception. I proudly danced on the open-aired dance floor, introducing her to Bert and Marietta, making small talk. A couple of times that evening I caught glances coming our way from my former best mate while the usually bubbling Marietta seemed rather more subdued.

The old year was giving way to the brash youngster of 1954. Everyone had made certain of having a glass with which to drink the new year in. I was the exception, still getting a couple of refills from the bar as the countdown began. As the electricity surged around the club many held their partners, ready to seal the new year with a kiss. I pushed through the crush toward Marcia, drinks in my hands. I reached her as 1954 pushed 1953 aside. Amid the cheering, laughter and singing I held Marcia close. We searched each other's faces silently. There was sadness as well as joy for us that night.

I remember an afternoon at Marcia's place. The England cricket side was touring the West Indies, playing this day at Sabina Park in Kingston. I sat by the radio listening to the duel taking place not so very far from where I sat in Marcia's bedroom. The great Len Hutton was opening the batting for England, probably with Cyril Washbrook. I wanted to stay glued to the radio. Marcia, bored with cricket, would have been far happier doing other things. She talked of having met the England team at a function some time before. It has to be said that over the years the question crossed my mind: did she get to know one of the players exceptionally well? This tour to the West Indies featured a young, brash player, the fiery Freddy Trueman, just beginning his years of greatness. His antics and bluntness of speech alarmed many of the traditional followers of the game. Although I did not see England in this series I had visited Sabina Park just once, to watch the West Indies take on India. I was amazed by the shouts from the huge crowd, a crowd restricted behind wire fences, almost cages. The noise was deafening. The players were more like gladiators playing in a cauldron threatening to explode in the event of any ill-considered judgment by the umpires. What pressure on these men, in a game a million miles away from the village green games of old England. How the West Indians love their cricket!

It was a time in the West Indies when a popular calypso told the story of the famous spin twins Rahmadin and Valentine bowling out England at Lords. The song, 'Cricket, Lovely Cricket' told of the wondrous deeds performed in that game. It was often accompanied by the steel drums that are such a characteristic part of the music of the West Indies.

My time with Marcia dwindled towards 1 March, St David's Day. Preparations were well in hand for the battalion to leave the island in a few weeks. As New Year's Eve had had a special meaning for me, so again did the last St David's Day I would know as a member of the Royal Welch Fusiliers. Out with Marcia, I had too much to drink and began acting rather the worse for wear, being unpleasant to her. As I walked with her towards her house I had a brush with a couple of local youths who said something to which I took exception. In a drunken act of foolishness I ran after them as they walked away. I picked up some small rocks to toss after them, with Marcia standing helplessly watching my stupidity. The rocks bounced along the road past the retreating Jamaicans who ignored me and moved off into the night. I now think that I was fortunate that they did not set on me and give me a hiding. Marcia and I had a scene over the incident that turned ugly and climaxed as I stormed off to camp. I would see Marcia just once more after this. As I staggered and swayed my way through the night my alcohol-clouded brain told me that I did not care if this was the last time I would see her. I was going home to cinema queues in rainy streets, to fish and chips drenched in vinegar, to friendly pubs with warm beer that frothed invitingly, to virgin Welsh girls with sing-song accents. I would be returning to frost and snow, with Christmas lights and Christmas trees glowing in lighted windows. I would see again lit-up buses coming out of the rain to take me to a football match, to scream abuse at a referee, usually English. So ended St David's Day.

And now our days were full of activity, with excitement buzzing in the air. Orders came thick and fast on the dos and don'ts of the battalion's move. I had a locked suitcase under my bed, packed with presents for my family. They included a bottle of Captain Morgan rum, bought for around ten shillings but worth a great deal more in Britain. I unpacked my uniform for cold climates and gave it a good airing. I found it threadbare in patches. I could have applied for a new one but didn't consider it worth the trouble seeing that I would soon be leaving the Army.

I did not see Marcia during these last days. With my thoughts full of going home I was able to push her behind a door in my mind. Now and then the door would open enough for me to be aware that she was there but I would hastily give the door a kick and think of the voyage to come. The date we were to leave Jamaica was given as 11 March. The Duke of Cornwall's Light Infantry, the DCLI, would relieve us. Its advance party arrived on the *Empire Clyde*, a troopship formerly known as the *Cameronia*. The ship that was to take us home had continued to Belize to complete the change-over there before returning to Jamaica. Many of us were amazed when watching the soldiers of the DCLI carrying out their rapid light infantry drill. Everything was done at the quick-time and to us verged on the comical. But by tradition that was the way things were done in the light infantry.

With only days to go I reflected on my three years away.

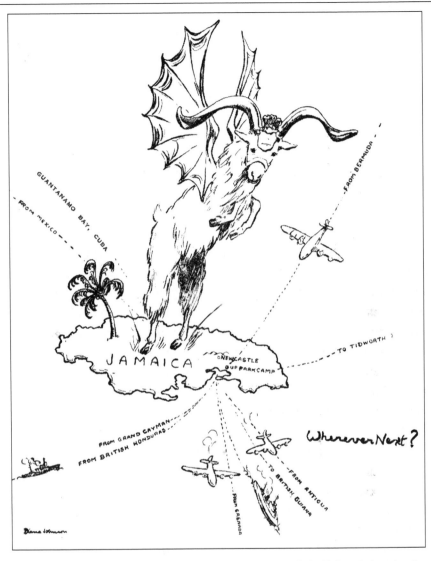

A souvenir of the Royal Welch's Caribbean tour, with 'Billy' and the island of Jamaica: 'wherever next?'

16

Jamaica farewell

If my memory serves me all other ranks were confined to camp that final night. However I am sure that the order was broken and that many farewells took place around Kingston, with men using the initiative that the army had tried to foster in them. The army created a paradox here, requiring instant obedience to orders no matter what. I did not attempt to make my way out of camp to seek out Marcia. For me that chapter was at an end, or so I thought. Even at the very end of our tour, the old women with deep lines etched on their dark faces still sold Jamaican souvenirs outside the camp swimming pool. We now left them and it for the pale-skinned soldiers who were about to take over from us. The coloured workers at the NAAFI might miss friendships built over time with some of us but only for a short while. They would grow into the culture of a new regiment and make friends with men with the accents of the south-west of England. Then it would all happen again as these new friends would leave too. But not for long now: the push for Jamaican independence was gaining momentum. The days of colonialism were ending. The Fusiliers' rush to Belize had been about the last gasp of gunboat diplomacy. The British lion was becoming feeble. There was in 1982 a grand gesture to snarl and show claws again but that was mostly to salvage the career of a desperate Margaret Thatcher. For all the skill of the Task Force it was the death rattle of Britain as an imperial power.

Times are changing. For a time there was open discussion of Britain turning away from the monarchy. The idea of fighting for Queen and Country might have a hollow ring to it in an age when people are much better informed. In the early 'fifties we accepted much more. We did not question, especially as soldiers of the Queen. Brought up on Britain's great historical triumphs and on victories – however costly – in two world wars, we glowed with pride as members of the Royal Welch Fusiliers, revelling in its proud traditions. For us the enemy was always black, our Queen and Country bathed in a white light. Now, with the mystique stripped away from the royal family and the corruption of those in high places exposed, perhaps many are not so keen to follow blindly as we once were. With the reality of war seen on television from Vietnam many have lost the creed 'my country right or wrong'. Even though much of the Gulf War were concealed by careful management of the media, many all over the globe saw that the conflict was more to do with oil than the ideals of freedom and democracy.

How I enjoyed that last breakfast at Up Park camp. There was a surreal air about the camp and cookhouse as we lined up for our meal as we had done so often in the past three years. We ate and then washed our utensils in the large tank of hot water outside the cookhouse and rinsed them an adjoining tank of cleaner water. Then it was back to our barrack blocks for the final clean up, including the toilet blocks. Even on such a day – or because of it – the army did not intend to lower its standards. Just as the outgoing tenant leaves a clean house behind so the Royal Welch Fusiliers pursued the highest traditions but with a broom rather than a gun. There seemed to be a joy in sweeping floors, cleaning windows and scrubbing toilets. We folded our bedding and returned it to the company store, where blankets and sheets were checked off. I had been done over by a storeman at Catterick early in my army career. On handing in my bedding an old soldier told me that I was missing a pillow cover, I think. I insisted that I had never been given one, only to be shown that it was included on the sheet bearing my signature. The storeman gave me the option of paying for it – I think seven shillings and sixpence – or be put on a report when I could expect to appear before an officer and be punished and have the cost of the item deducted from my pay. Being raw in the ways of the army I handed over the cash to avoid further trouble and probably paid for the storeman's beer that evening. Of course the storeman had merely inserted a figure 1 in the column opposite 'pillow cover' to add to the articles I had actually received and signed for. I wonder how many times he had pulled the trick on rookies. The obvious way to avoid such ploys was to insist on a line being drawn through columns that did not apply. But in 1954 at Up Park camp I returned my bedding without a hitch.

It was time for our last parade. Then we boarded lorries that we expected to take us to the docks of Kingston. Instead we were delivered to a patch of ground somewhere in the city where were left to our own devices for some considerable time. We sat in groups, smoking and talking before again boarding vehicles and heading for the docks. As we passed through the city streets, as busy as ever, we waved our farewells through the canvas archway of our truck. Some responded to our waves, others did not. Many gave us wide smiles, exclaiming 'bye Welsh!' Giggling girls waved exaggeratedly as we gave out wolf whistles. Then we were in the dock area, evident from the dirtier streets, run-down buildings and above all the hint of salt in the morning air. We strained our necks to catch a first glimpse of the *Empire Clyde*, urged on by the screeching seagulls doing aerobatics above us. The ship looked impressive to us as we paraded on the dockside. Most of us probably would not have cared if she had been a banana boat but seeing that the voyage would be a three-week one it was good to have some comfort.

The crowd at the dockside grew bigger by the minute, a mixture of civilians and soldiers. After the usual delay we trooped up the gangway to establish ourselves on board. We followed the same pattern as we had on the *Dilwara* three years before. As men laid claim to their sleeping berths and deposited their kit, they drifted up to the main decks to wait for the ship's departure. There were many people on the wharf now, each with a special friend or friends to farewell, heads back looking at the troops swarming over the *Empire Clyde*. As I peered down I heard a soldier on my left calling my name and pointing for me to look down at a particular section of the crowd. I followed his pointing finger, my eyes suddenly resting on Marcia smiling up at me. She looked most attractive, carrying a rosy red apple in each hand. Strange as it may seem, apples were a luxury in Jamaica and most expensive to buy. With the noise all around, Welsh voices soaring out in song and a band below it was beyond hope that Marcia and I could have any sort of a conversation. She made signs that she wanted me to have the apples and that she was about to throw them. I held out my arms to catch them only to see them pass to my left. A couple of lads who had been watching plucked the fruit out of the air and threw them to me. I waved them for Marcia to see, her face both sad

'On the way at last': the troopship *Empire Clyde*, the postcard 'Tommy' sent to 'Dear Dad & Family' on leaving Jamaica.

and happy. Suddenly I could feel the ship sliding away from the dockside, as we at last got under way. I stood looking at Marcia, apples clutched in my hands, as she and the rest of the crowd moved toward the edge of the wharf to make up the distance between them and the ship if only for a few moments. She waved and smiled as I stood on the deck gazing down at her for many minutes. Then the jumble of faces, colours and shapes began to blur into one mass as the ship moved away and it was no longer possible to recognize anyone farewelling us. The figures remained on the wharf as we moved along the beautiful harbour in the afternoon sun, with the long finger of land alongside keeping us for a while longer in contact with the island. Then we passed the end of the Palisadoes peninsula and passed out into the open sea. Jamaica had passed out of my life. I wrote to Marcia, and she to me, for about six months after leaving Jamaica. But life goes on and I eventually walked down other avenues, and down the aisle with someone else.

Many of us remained on the deck of the ship watching the island fade into the afternoon haze until it was no longer visible. The steady drone of the ship's engines told us that the first stage of our voyage, back to Bermuda, was well and truly beginning. We stayed to watch the ship sail into the orange and dusky blue colours of evening. I then put my apples in a safe place. I kept them for a few days before deciding to eat them. It would have been good if I could have kept the fruit pristine to recall Marcia in the future but everything has its season and the apples demanded to be devoured. They tasted good, the first apples I had eaten for many months. They were both a peace offering and a farewell. I was glad that she had come to the wharf and that we had parted with a smile: I thought a lot of that.

I believe it may have been the next morning after leaving Kingston that I saw Elvira. I was on deck doing nothing in particular when I caught sight of her petite figure standing alone looking out to sea. She was on a part of the deck out of bounds to unmarried soldiers. But I am certain it was her and I gazed at her out of the corners of my eyes until unexpectedly our eyes connected. For ten seconds we looked at each other before I looked away. She was now the wife of another Fusilier on her way to a new life in a new country. She was a part of the life I had left behind over the horizon but I must admit to feeling some pangs of regret. I knew that she had seen and recognised me and I wondered about her true thoughts. She was leaving her mother far behind in Belize to spend her days without her daughters, with Maria already gone with her Inniskilling. Perhaps one day the fare would arrive for their mother to join them. Perhaps mother and daughters would never meet again, the price the family had been prepared to pay for the daughters to get out of Belize. I ambled away from Elvira and never saw her again for the rest of the voyage. It was the last time I would ever see her. Despite the increase in weight and the appearance of sea-sickness she was still as pretty as ever.

The journey across the Atlantic was virtually a re-run of the voyage three years before. There were film shows. I can recall seeing Ethel Merman and Donald O'Connor in the breezy musical *Call Me Madam*. Ethel Merman's powerful voice drowned out even the thud-thud of the ship's engines. Once again the quality of the food rose above Army cooking and we looked forward to each meal, appetites sharpened by the sea air. The voyage aroused other appetites. We amused ourselves with stories about a woman on board – said to be a nurse – who was supposed to have spent a great deal of time with men inside one of the ship's covered lifeboats. We did not doubt that she was a nymphomaniac; whether it was true, I now wonder.

Bermuda came and was left behind. Unimpressed by the place in comparison to Jamaica I did not go ashore. We ventured out into the Atlantic and the skies changed to grey. The Atlantic gave way to home waters. We steamed up the Irish Sea, our land of Wales hidden in the murkiness of night. With the coming of a grey dawn the *Empire Clyde* docked at Liverpool. Through the portholes we could see signs of a familiar country, and hear dockhands speaking in Scouse accents. It seemed like a dream to be in Britain. With rationing over, the post-war drift into consumerism had begun. A new medium, television, was beginning to bring to the people messages of what they needed to have to be happy and to be ahead of their neighbours. Soon a Prime Minister, Harold Macmillan, would tell the nation that they had never had it so good.

We were to leave Liverpool by train for Swindon to a camp on the outskirts of Chiseldon, in Wiltshire. We found Chiseldon set in green fields, a model English village and as great a contrast with Jamaica as we could have. As we were taken by lorry along country roads past the vivid green of the fields everything seemed surreal: familiar and yet strange all at the same time. I was waiting to see bare black feet shuffling through the white dust of a Jamaican road, but it had turned into a smooth modern asphalt one. I looked out for the dhobi women carrying the washed, starched and folded washing on their heads, bottoms moving almost comically, black skin, pink only on palms and soles, expressive eyes; crinkly, wiry hair. But there were none, only a farmer leading his mare, a bossy-looking woman riding a bicycle and a couple of children slapping gloved fingers together to keep warm at a bus stop. Even the road signs pointed to strange places, not to familiar names such as Port Antonio, Morant Bay or Mandeville. Jamaica was with me still.

We reached the camp, where I was hoping to be granted leave immediately. But the Army was in no great rush and I spent the night at the camp. The next day turned out to be more promising, with leave passes and rail warrants issued. But another night would pass before I would finally board a bus for Swindon and the train to South Wales. I struggled with my suitcase containing my presents from Jamaica but was comforted by the feel of the wad of cash I had been given to spend on leave. I looked ahead to days of getting out of bed when it suited me rather than the Army. I thought of tall glasses of English beer and darts in a pub warmed by an open fire. I was full of expectation. At Swindon railway station I bought some magazines to read on the journey, finding a near-empty compartment bearing the names of the main stations of Wales on its side. I left the magazines unread, falling into a half-sleep, thoughts of the West Indies wandering through my mind.

The train at last entered Wales, stopping at Newport and then Cardiff. I felt the excitement well up inside me as the familiar landscape of my country unfolded through the grimy window. There were not so many fine houses now, but rows of houses, different only in their cosmetic paint. Chimneys sat on slate roofs, with blue-grey smoke telling of coal fires burning in grates below. Young boys played football in narrow streets, 'one sock up, one sock round the ankle', kicking a tennis ball at a lanky youth keeping goal between a lamppost and a stone in the center of the road. With no crossbar and one post liable to shift by the force of a shot disputed goals would be usual. As the train moved away I saw 'one sock up, one sock round the ankle' standing still, following a desperate save by the lanky one, hands on hips in disgust at a missed goal. I saw factories spewing their wastes into the sky over the valleys and slag heaps that told of brave miners, soon to become a dying breed. From the train I saw hoardings advertising products old and new, those Bisto children still dirty, sniffing at the aroma of gravy coming their way. The television aerials were not as prolific as I had noticed in Liverpool but the march was on, gaining by the day. Friendly-looking telephone boxes in bright red paint waited in the streets for cold windy nights when teenagers would huddle inside to keep warm rather than stay at home with parents and glowing coal fires. Yes, this was my Wales, of Saturday nights of overflowing pubs and overflowing beer. Where those who had toiled through a long week and found fame with a song or two, protesting – half-heartedly – before accepting the crowd's call to take center-stage. This was the Wales where rugby remained a religion, challenging the chapels, with beating England the Holy Grail. This land of high mountains and deep valleys, of princes and battles long gone: I was home.

So my leave of almost three months began. I bought a civilian suit, only to discover that pin stripes had become hopelessly out of fashion in the meantime. I returned to wearing my somewhat threadbare uniform. Going to dances around Swansea I was soon to learn how little I had in common with the girls I met. If I steered the conversation around to Jamaica, feeling like a well-travelled man-of-the-world hero – they would look completely uninterested, saying something bland like 'that's nice'. I sensed that some of these young women had little idea where Jamaica was, thinking that the West Indies were somewhere off the coast of India. Here there were no sensuous calypsos, only foxtrots, quicksteps and the Flirtation Barn Dance. This last dance became the highlight of the evening, with its easy steps giving access to many potential partners. I had the sensation not of having returned from a long journey but of never having made it. I was still mentally back in Jamaica even though physically I was in Wales. I did not feel a part of Swansea in 1954 and all the expectations I had held about returning home seemed to collapse in a heap. Somehow the reality of being in Britain did not seem as good as the longing to be there.

The time arrived to return to Chiseldon to do some more soldiering. Preparations were well in hand for the big parade in July when our new young Queen would present the battalion with new Colours. There were many drill parades leading to the big occasion, with everyone conscious of the importance of the day and the regiment's reputation. For me this was to be the grand finale of my Army career. When the big day arrived all went well, with the Royal Welch Fusiliers sharp in their drill and proud of their march past the Queen. I was surprised to see how young and attractive the Queen appeared (she was about four years older than me) and how relaxed was the security when I saw her pass by. She walked a few feet away from me. But those were the days before the assassination of John F. Kennedy when the world, as well as America, lost its innocence. The celebrations did not end with the parade. The Queen visited our camp and attended a dinner in the Officers' Mess with all officers proudly wearing their medals on full dress uniforms.

Since my return I had been introduced to television. The first program I had seen featured a blonde-haired youngster strumming a guitar and singing in a pleasant cockney voice, a young Tommy Steele at the onset of his career. That summer the World Cup was played in Europe. We marveled that some of the games would be shown live on television. A television set was provided so we could watch some games while off duty. Even in black and white the event for us in camp was spectacular.

Queen Elizabeth II addressing the Royal Welch's parade at Chiseldon, July 1954,
Tom's final ceremonial duty in the army.

It was about this time that I visited Swansea for the weekend, returning late on Sunday evening. I managed to stay awake for most of the journey, only to drop off as the train neared my destination. Through bleary eyes I saw the word SWINDON on a station sign as the train moved out, gathering speed. Panic swept over me as I debated whether I should pull the communication cord and risk a fine. On long reflection since I feel I should have pulled the chord and risked the fine. As the train got up more speed and left Swindon further behind I decided to sit tight, go on to the next station and try to get back to Swindon by another train. Providing I could reach camp by the beginning of the day I would escape any penalty: the memory of my lucky escape in Kingston must have fuelled my anxiety. The train seemed to go on and on: would it stop before London? It eventually stopped with a fierce jerk at a place I cannot now remember – perhaps Didcot. I was out of the coach like a rocket, my first task being to find someone to whom to explain my situation. There was also the worry of having to pay for the extra journey: perhaps it would have been cheaper to have pulled the communication cord, I thought. But all was well. There was a train passing through Swindon, giving me a chance to make camp in time. What was more, the railway men were sympathetic and let me travel back to Swindon without charge. But there was time to kill before the train arrived, time spent on a chilly station platform, huddled on a wooden bench. It was hard to keep my eyes from closing despite the cold and the discomfort: I was terrified of missing the train. Time passed slowly on a deserted platform until the Swindon train pulled in, miraculously, on time. In the end I made it back to camp by a whisker. All that Monday I was congratulating myself for having got out of bringing my Army career to a close in disgrace.

I was now counting the days to my release. I turned down the commanding officer's invitation to sign on for further service and go to Germany with the battalion. The urge for further adventure was still with me but weighed against having to serve for another three years. I resisted the temptation. And so a short time later, leaving the Army a week early thanks to a corrupt clerk whose price was thirty shillings, I passed into civilian life.

My memories of my tour to the West Indies have stayed with me always even if the details have sometimes faded. It all happened a long time ago. Perhaps it was not of great importance on a broader scale, but it was important to me. How clearly I can recall those twinkling lights of Kingston from the darkness of a Newcastle night, high in the Blue Mountains. I can see again the buildings running down the mountainside, the dim lighting of the camp highlighting the bright illumination of the barrack rooms. All is silent but for the bullfrogs on the mountainside and the dive-bombing of insects flying around in the blackness. The soldiers in the graveyard sleep on caressed by the cool breeze, their duty done forever. I wonder now if the badge of the Royal Welch Fusiliers has joined those sculpted into the big wall behind the guns, joining those of the regiments that went before. I can see the streets of Kingston, teeming with life on a Saturday night. Soldiers with money jingling in civilian trousers searching for a place to taste the rum and more besides. From open-fronted clubs and milk bars come the strains of calypsos, filling the street with tunes like 'Please Mister Don't You Touch My Tomato'. Men from all over the world – sailors from Germany, Norway and Britain – roam the streets, out for a good time. There are pimps there too, telling of girls who will go all night, and where they can be bought. Like any city anywhere, perhaps, yet special for me, lost in the time warp of the early nineteen-fifties. The soldiers who walked those bustling streets are for me forever young. In my memory they will never grow old. The Fusiliers I remember will never know greying hair or baldness, the slowing of the limbs, the fading of the eyes. In my memory we march in youth once again, Colours flying in the sun, a stirring Welsh tune to heat the blood and raise the head just a little higher.

Tom and Kay, courting in
Mumbles soon after their
engagement, 1955.

A family portrait, Wales, just before
leaving for Australia, around 1965.

Printed in Australia
AUOC02n0741220715
269064AU00001B/1/P